The Film Guide to God

TIM CAWKWELL

DARTON·LONGMAN + TODD

First published in 2004 by
Darton, Longman and Todd Ltd
1 Spencer Court
140–142 Wandsworth High Street
London SW18 4JJ

ISBN 0–232–52466–1

A catalogue record for this book is available from the British Library.

All biblical quotations are taken from the Authorised Version
unless otherwise stated.

Designed by Sandie Boccacci
Phototypeset in 9.5/13.75pt Stone Serif
by Intype Libra Ltd
Printed and bound in Great Britain by
The Cromwell Press, Trowbridge, Wiltshire

Contents

Acknowledgements

I would like to thank a number of people for help in the preparation of this book: Sarah Knight for her careful reading of the text; the Reverend Douglas Brown for comment on the chapter 'The Image of Christ'; members of my family for their advice and encouragement, my children Katy and Thomas and especially my wife Maggie; Penny Banks for help in word processing; my editors at Darton, Longman and Todd, Katie Worrall and Virginia Hearn; and those who attended the classes held under the title 'The Filmgoer's Guide to God' at the Norwich Cathedral Institute, the discussions from which led to the writing of this book.

TIM CAWKWELL
timcawkwell@hotmail.com
Norwich, April 2003

|

Prologue

You're in the jailhouse now.
Jimmie Rodgers, 'In the Jailhouse'

I have never been to prison, but I have spent time in Alcatraz. On 27 November 2002, I visited the rock of Alcatraz in San Francisco Bay, toured the prison block of the former federal penitentiary and even stopped inside a cell in a feeble attempt to experience a whiff of that solitude which must come from living in a bounded space. My thought was of the ancient hermits who *chose* such confinement as a way of getting closer to God. The writing of this book then seemed to come into focus. Several of the films I had written about featured life in prison in some way or other: *O Brother, Where Art Thou?*; *Sullivan's Travels*; *The Night of the Hunter*; *Pickpocket*; *American Gigolo*; *Rome, Open City*; *The Army in the Shadows*; *A Man Escaped*; *The Passion of Joan of Arc* and *Accattone*. Even the crux of the gospel story concerns an innocent man brought before his interrogators and kept in a prison overnight before being executed. To visit Alcatraz and stand inside a cell seemed for a moment to bring me closer to my subject.

The fact that Alcatraz is now an enormous tourist attraction gives a macabre twist to the contemporary taste for theme parks. Our human solidarity makes us fascinated with the mechanics of denying freedom to our fellow human beings. Then the thought creeps in: who is being denied? Certainly the homicides banged up in their cells, and probably the warders who have to guard them day and night, imprisoned as it were in the grinding routine of their duties: what difference between the incarcerated inmates and the guard on sentry duty in his own confined space, rifle at the ready for any sign of infraction? But might we latter-day visitors also be locked into solitary for an hour, wandering round like automata, transfixed to our audio headsets? The thought comes back to me: we are born free but everywhere we are in prison.

For the religious person, freedom is found in the company of God, in the spiritual life not the material one. Human justice is riddled with error, imperfection and corruption, an idea we shall encounter in a number of films: the gospel story of Jesus' trial and death, in the versions of Dostoevsky's *Crime and Punishment*, in the stories of wartime occupation, in the story of the martyrdom of Joan of Arc. Yet to portray existence lived behind mental bars, neither prison nor the vagaries of human authority are necessary: the protagonists of *Diary of a Country Priest*, *Winter Light*, *Under Satan's Sun*, *Nostalgia*, *Andrei Rublev*, *Stalker*, *The Apostle*, *Brighton Rock*, *The Funeral* and *The Word* all wrestle to a greater or lesser intensity with what human freedom means. In this context, compassion and the capacity to imagine divinely created abundance are the softeners of pain, the human capacities that mitigate the harshness of existence, as witnessed by *Mouth Agape*, *Mother and Son*, *The Nantes Triptych*, *Babette's Feast* and *Breaking the Waves*.

In choosing which films to write about, I have confined myself to those made in Europe (interpreted as including Russia and Georgia) and the United States of America, and the God in question is the Christian one, not the Islamic, Jewish or any other kind of God. That is deliberate, in order to preserve a focus to the theme. My aim has been to give an introduction to religious cinema for those with a general interest in religious art and literature, but I hope also that, since the analysis derives from careful and repeated study of the works themselves, those who like films before they are interested in religion will find new insights. The book strives to make plain that it is the visual thrust that distinguishes film from literary narrative, so that framing, movement and editing are key to the understanding of the artifice of film, artifice being understood as the process that embodies creativity of thought, of giving form to ideas. The libretto is important in opera but it is the music to which it is set that stamps it with dramatic power. An intelligent script is important in film, but it is the creative succession of images that makes a film capable of repeated viewing and that unfolds its power which, like that of opera, is not necessarily experienced to the full on an initial encounter.

In selecting what films to write about, another choice has been important as well. Religion in film has two poles: at one end the strict biblical film, at the other *any* film which deals with the ideas central to a Christian understanding of the universe, such as redemption, humility, compassion, unexpected salvation, paradise. While I have engaged with the biblical wing in terms of films of the gospel, hardly to be avoided in a book of this title, I have not entered the vast territory of the other wing, for fear of going nowhere in particular. Instead my goal has been to explore a specific terrain, namely those films which engage with the meaning and purpose of human existence as it might be found in faith in a trinitarian, Christian God. Cinema is a global art form and when one thinks of the huge number of films that have been made in the past 100 years or so, I have only dealt with a tiny handful. Yet it is a mighty one too. A number of remarkable works of art have emerged from this cross-fertilisation of the centuries-old reflection on the nature of the Christian God and the century-old art of the cinema and four quintessentially cinematic minds have achieved masterpieces from the use of religious stories: the Frenchman Robert Bresson, the Dane Carl Theodor Dreyer, the Italian Roberto Rossellini, and the Russian Andrei Tarkovsky.

One very significant difference exists between them and

Christian artists from before the Italian Renaissance: we know their names, since the Renaissance itself created a wider sense of society so that builders, sculptors, painters etc. won a record for themselves, escaping from the anonymity of their predecessors. Furthermore, we are heirs of Romanticism, which gave the artist a heroic status as interpreter of the world, a repository of truth often in opposition to authority seeking to corrupt it. The names and ideas of these creators therefore become even more important. Modern atheism has a variety of sources: not just the Enlightenment, not just Darwinism, but also the deep distrust of institutional authority. In seeking someone to cling to, we turn instead to individual interpreters of the world for answers about existence and God. The cinema at this point is in a position of privilege, for the early film-makers (Carl Dreyer is an example) had to create afresh a cinematic language and the means for telling a religious story. If there was a temptation to take the death of God as the beginning of cinema, they did not necessarily succumb to it. Instead they held in their hands a new means of asking the religious questions. At the same time, there has been a tendency to create a gap between religious authority and the film-maker. With Rossellini, after a lifetime of making Catholicism an unproblematic strand in a number of films including a version of the gospel story (*The Messiah*), this dissidence caused him to assert that he was a 'religious atheist', in other words that he was willing to take on the ideas of Christianity in all their creative potency provided this did not include a belief in God.

Indeed a spectre stalks this feast, that of Communism, the creed of 'scientific atheism', the vogue for which among intellectuals and creative artists made religious faith suspect. The death of God proclaimed in the nineteenth century encouraged revolutionaries to find some other millennial solution to the sufferings of the world. Hence the spread of Marxist thought in the twentieth century, which in an artist like Pier Paolo Pasolini produced the most extraordinary results. From his pen and from his camera came work which in turn (and occasionally at the same time) recoiled in disgust at the world, scorned authority of any kind, found among the poor, especially the rural poor, a capacity for the mystical which affluence and technocracy were squeezing out, and sought in a condition of human crisis the revolutionary movement, most notably and unexpectedly in *The Gospel According to St Matthew,* the inflammatory life and words of Jesus Christ.

Nor was it just Marxism that might draw a thinking film-maker to its side. The growth of western philosophies from which God had been thoroughly excised was a similar attraction. Hence it seemed to me worthwhile to follow a *via negativa,* as it were, and look at the films of the godless Frenchman Jean-Pierre Melville. In part a product of existentialist circles in France, Melville devised a world in which the gangster became a mythical hero in the absence of any divine law governing the universe, and I contrast him with Robert Bresson, a similar product of existentialism, who took a contrary route: a sense of meaninglessness could only be redeemed by the act of believing. Enter the Swede, Ingmar Bergman, a contemporary of these two film-makers, who squared the circle by taking an intense interest in the concept of faith and at the same time locating in God an utter heartlessness.

The horrors of the twentieth century, the century of total war, of genocide, and of utter cynicism, form a backdrop to this book. To counterbalance this pain, art has never seemed more important, offering as it does a way to transcend this mental imprisonment, namely the opportunity to see it from the outside and as distant, not unlike a contemporary tourist visiting an infamous prison like Alcatraz. The pleasures of the cinema can help us for it is as good an art form as any to celebrate the lyrical moment, to provide erotic thrills, to trumpet the triumphal moment in epic grandeur, to unite image, word and music in a grand synthesis that would out-strip even Wagner's *Götterdämmerung.* Yet none of these things are found at the centre of this book. Instead we are looking at stories, often very simple, about people, stories filtered through the cinematic sensibility, and in Dreyer, Bresson and Tarkovsky, through the most delicate manipulators of visual, as opposed to verbal narrative that the twentieth century was able to produce. These fictions return to some essence of human existence, how people manifest compassion for each other, how they transcend a sin such as pride, how they receive unexpected grace, how some redemptive circumstance can heal the human consciousness of meaningless suffering. The journey at times is unrelieved and only after the confrontation for many of the protagonists with sin, failure and death, as it were like Samson (Judges 16) who 'did grind in the prison house' and then 'bowed himself with all his might' in order to find release, do I make place for two particular films, *The Colour of Pomegranates* and *Francis, God's Jester*, that express a religious ideal which finds sacredness in creation and in each present moment. The religious life is not a means of bearing the burden but a celebration of the world. Briefly therefore, we on earth find ourselves in heaven.

2

God's Grace and God's Silence

I wake and feel the fell of dark not day.
G. M. Hopkins, Sonnet ('I wake . . .')

This book concludes with a consideration of gospel films, of how film-makers have treated the supreme Christian narrative in which all the themes present in the films discussed – compassion, transcendence, grace, salvation, redemption – dominate that particular story and indeed drive it to its conclusion. We start with three parish priests in three films, representatives of Christ on earth, striving to convey his teaching and to practise his love. In choosing to be priests, they seek to become saints, but all three wrestle with weakness and sinfulness within and without them. One triumphs, one fails, the third seems to attain to a diabolical version of sainthood.

Two particular film directors need to be brought centre stage in any discussion of how the cinema in the twentieth century has approached religion: the Frenchman Robert Bresson and the Swede Ingmar Bergman. Both emerge from a heroic tradition of European culture that poses questions about the existence of God and of morality and of what it means to be human. Many writers have discussed Ingmar Bergman and his films exercised a particular fascination for those who sought a serious version of cinema away from the commercial environment of film-making and film-going. Bergman became a paragon of film art and of how the important questions of life should be asked. Christianity entered his bloodstream at birth because his father was a Protestant pastor. If the film scripted by Bergman and based on his parents' courtship and marriage, *The Best Intentions*, is any guide, family life was an intense and oppressive affair. In truth as Bergman grew older, he so expunged Christianity from his mind that by the end of his film career its comforts amount to nothing. An interview with Bergman in the late 1960s, covering his whole film-making career up to then, sees him taking the view that Christianity is 'deeply branded by a very virulent humiliation motif', that 'Protestantism is a wretched kettle of fish', that the Christian God might be 'something destructive and fantastically dangerous, something filled with risk for the human body and bringing out in him dark destructive forces instead of the opposite'. The epitome of these ideas is the terrifying portrait of Bishop Edvard Vergerus, the puritanical stepfather in *Fanny and Alexander*, a summation of Bergman's deep hatred of the idea of fatherhood, whether divine or human. Yet Bergman is intriguing for he does not appear to dispute that God exists, just that he is loving. It may be for this reason that he draws audiences suffering from a crisis of faith, since he allows them to keep their God but at the same time to dislike him or even blame him.

Robert Bresson is different. An intellectual by nature, immersed in Pascal, Dostoevsky and Bernanos, he responded to the post-war philosophy of existentialism during the 1950s and 60s by adapting it to his Catholicism, yet in doing so succeeded in appealing firmly to that same generation of filmgoers (if not the same ones) for whom Bergman offered some secret solution to life. He managed to do this in three ways: by the philosophical quality of his stories since they all deal intensely with human free will, by adopting an unorthodox even heretical approach since he was preoccupied with the virtues of suicide, and finally by the manner of his story telling. He used close-ups, off-screen sound and ellipses in order to compose his films with a rigour rare in the commercial cinema.

His Catholicism in particular drew on Georges Bernanos (1888–1948), a French novelist who sought to explode the comfortable traditions of the Church with scorching notions of salvation and grace. In 1950, in his third film, Bresson's style came of age when he chose to make a version of Bernanos' *Journal d'un curé de campagne/Diary of a Country Priest* (hereafter *Journal*). Although the book is densely written, Bresson brilliantly achieves a fidelity to the narrative while compressing its long speeches and dialogues, and to its mood. For the latter, he uses music more extensively than in subsequent work and in the 1950s it seems to have been the one area of his film style that remained for him to purge. After this film, he used only snatches from the classical composers, Mozart, Schubert, Monteverdi etc., and then for his last four films dropped music altogether.

One feature of Jean-Jacques Grünenwald's score in *Journal* is its uneasiness, at places conveying anxiety in the same way that Debussy did in his opera, *Pelléas et Mélisande*. This fits the story well: the priest arrives at his first parish and becomes enmeshed in conflict with the family in the big house. The Count is having an affair with the governess Louise, the Countess has retreated from the family into an obsessional devotion to the memory of her son who died young and Chantal, the teenage daughter, has been moved by her parents' lovelessness to a despair issuing in jealousy of Louise and to cultivating a poisonous air of malice. The film's central scene involves the young priest wrestling with the soul of the Countess, forcing her to find peace in God's will rather than rebel against it. He wins but when the Countess dies that night, released from her years of pain, his torment intensifies because the family, prompted by Chantal's malice, interprets the priest's conversation between the two, which was in effect a confession and therefore subject to a code of complete privacy, as a chastisement of the Countess by the priest which breaks her will to live. The film ends with the fragile priest going to see the doctor in Lille, being diagnosed as having stomach cancer, taking shelter with his seminary friend Dufrety who had thrown up the priesthood, and dying in his down-at-heel apartment, although not before he has gone 'soul to soul' with Dufrety to urge him to go back to the priesthood. The film ends with Dufrety agreeing to see the curé de Torcy and with the priest's last reported words, 'What does it matter? All is grace.'

This sequence at Lille that lasts a little over quarter of an hour, effective though it is, is essentially a coda to the main story, which is the battle of wills between the priest and Chantal. The chief climax comes after some 90 minutes when Chantal visits the priest as he proposes to leave for Lille. She has got her way in the big house, for Louise is to depart, but, having previously eavesdropped on the conversation with her mother, she admits to him that he effected a miracle with the Countess in drawing her out of her resignation into a state of peace.

Grünenwald's score echoes the claustrophobia of the big house, which only this choirboy of a priest, emitting a sort of incandescence ('un espèce de feu qui les brûle'), is able to purge. This shifting music finds a counterpart in the way Bresson tells the story. Bernanos' original novel certainly focuses on the conflict between priest and family, so intense as to place it on a mystic plane, but Bresson uses the techniques of film to create a quite other dimension to the tensions of the story. To give an example, Louise the governess is often the only communicant at the priest's early-morning Mass but after the priest receives an anonymous letter telling him to leave the parish, by chance he finds it matches the writing in a prayer book that has been left behind in church. He places the book on a chair and while the camera remains fixed on it, we hear footsteps off-screen of someone coming to Mass: Bresson is telling us we are about to discover the author of the letter. It turns out to be the faithful Louise. This device of steps being heard off-screen is a standard means in the cinema of creating suspense, quite absent from the novel.

For any priest coming to a parish with a squire, the relationship between church and big house is crucial, potentially a microcosm of relations between Church and State. The Count has the barn which the priest wants to convert into a youth club. Will he give it or will he block his ideas? Early on the Count does 'approve all the plans' but then tells the priest to go very slowly on the grounds that the parish is difficult: the young man's idealism comes brutally up against the older man's cynicism. Other events soon overtake these negotiations: the young priest, having failed to use an opportunity to reproach the town clerk for his late-night dances which he believes are corrupting the youth of the village, shortly after does not shrink from reproving the Count for the unhappiness of his daughter.

This frosty conversation comes as a turning point. After it, the priest is engaged in spiritual combat for the rest of the film and his suffering moves up a gear, as it were. But prior to it, Bresson produces a marvellously deft picture of the rural priest's lot, specific to a tiny Catholic parish in northern France but with a universal quality as well. First Fabregars, 'baptised in vinegar' (as a parishioner was once described to me), remonstrates that he is being overcharged for his wife's funeral and that the church is battening on the misery of the poor; the priest seeks advice from the older curé de Torcy who lectures him that he should have kicked Fabregars out for his meanness, that in his day they made 'chefs de paroisses' and now they send choirboys, who 'whinge instead of command', who want to be loved when in fact 'a true priest is never loved'. Torcy then delivers some cruel advice on the parochial ministry: 'Create order all day long. Do it thinking that disorder will blow it all away.'

In the next shot we see the priest at home peeling potatoes, the man of sorrows in torment, interrupted when the town clerk arrives to tell him that the commune has agreed to have electricity installed in his house. Overcome with gratitude he refrains from saying anything about the late-night dances. The next shot shows the priest awake in the darkness listening to the noise of revelry coming from the square below. In a voice-over, the priest calls it a dreadful night ('nuit affreuse') and in the early morning light, he looks out of his window in his celibate solitude: 'I would have given anything for a word of comfort.' We hear but do not see a farm wagon moving off at dawn. Throughout the film, wagons are glimpsed or their presence is betrayed by the sound of wheels turning, as though they were the excruciating wheels of eternity under the grinding of which the priest suffers.

Bresson uses the priest's insomnia to make visible his wrestling with faith and loss of faith. The priest experiences Torcy's strictures at first hand when he learns from him that 'night may overturn all you achieve, for that is the order of things'. The priest's insomnia is shown six times, Bresson subtly using each occasion to mark the progress of his faith. The first, second and third occasions mark a progress into despair, so that by the third he can no longer pray; he prostrates himself but still finds the 'same silence'. Yet on the fourth occasion, his discovery that his faith still remains endows him with the strength to confront the crisis by engaging with the Countess on behalf of God. On the fifth occasion he learns of the Countess' death; on the sixth, following a dressing-down from the Count, he realises that while her long trial is over, his is about to begin, payment extracted from the living for the peace of the dead. These night scenes lock the story into place. They become the moments at which the earthly drama between the priest and the Count's dysfunctional family meets with the spiritual drama of the priest's trial of faith.

A novel can afford to be expansive, but the two-hour narrative film needs to be exacting in ordering time and space. The film's depth derives from the concise stitching together of these layers. Another dimension is provided by the four conversations he has with Torcy, starting with his denunciation of the choirboys or 'va-nu-pieds' the seminaries are turning out and ending with Torcy calling him a 'terrific priest' ('un fameux petit prêtre') and asking for his blessing. Like the night scenes, these conversations contain their own dramatic progress.

Yet another layer is provided by suicide. Death pervades the film and not just death but a will to death. The Countess, released from her obsession with her lost son, dies in her bed. Baldly told, the event is melodramatic but it signals something deeper: that death is a release. The priest himself, confining himself to a diet of dry bread soaked in wine and a little fruit, drives himself to the spiritual limit marked by death and at the close of the film crosses it. Thirdly, Chantal is ready to commit suicide but is deterred from this by the priest's detection of her intentions. Finally, death in its most unrelieved form comes with that of Dr Delbende, briefly but potently sketched in the film. Torcy, concerned for the priest's health, recommends to his friend, Dr Delbende, that he examine him. Shortly after this, Delbende is found dead at the hands of his own shot-gun with the suspicion that it was not an accident. Since Delbende was, on his own admission, an atheist, he has died without grace. The thought seems to horrify the priest but Torcy is confident: 'He was a just man.' Not only just but he, Torcy and the priest are asserted to be three of a kind, ready to 'stand up' ('faire face') as if heaven is granted not to the faithful but to those willing to 'stand up'.

Bernanos could not have found a more faithful interpreter than Bresson of the idea of the priestly vocation as he saw it, a wrestling with human sinfulness to the limit of physical capability so that death when it comes is a moment of triumph. It is towards the end of the story that we hear the priest write in his diary that mornings are blest and when he has learnt of his stomach cancer, and has faced up to the prospect of death, his thoughts are of the freshness of morning, a moment of renewal after the long and dreadful night, a time of angels.

Ingmar Bergman said in an interview in 1968 that he was 'tremendously fond' of *Diary of a Country Priest*, especially the book and admitted that he had seen the film seven or eight times. Its influence was one of the starting-points for *Winter Light* of 1961, an awesomely dreary film about rural ministry, provided we understand with Bergman that 'the importance of the dreary in art must not be underestimated'.

Its Swedish title is *Nattvardsgästerna* which means 'the

communicants' (Nattvard: 'holy communion') and the film's opening sequence, lasting nine minutes, about a ninth of its total length, shows Pastor Thomas Ericsson conducting the service of Eucharist in a small country church. Five people come to the altar rail: the fisherman Jonas Persson and his wife Karin, the schoolteacher Märta, the parish clerk and an old woman. The film ends with evensong in another parish attended solely by Märta, the parish clerk and the organist. In the bulk of the film, Bergman explores in his characteristically earnest way the relationships between the pastor and four of those who had attended communion in the morning.

At the age of forty-three when he made *Winter Light* with over 20 years of theatre directing behind him and 23 films to his credit as a director, he had evolved a collaborative style of working with his actors that cast them again and again in different roles. In this practice he is diametrically opposed to Bresson. While the latter felt professional actors brought falsity, Bergman believes that the mark of a good actor is an ability to enter a role from the outside and make it their own: 'Actors are trained to express complexities.' Exemplary in this regard is Max von Sydow, who played for Bergman a series of tortured and broken characters over a period between 1956 and 1970. He approaches these parts with a subtle detachment, the same which allowed him in the midst of this sequence to play Christ in *The Greatest Story Ever Told* (see chapter 12) and lend something magnetic to that sprawling failure. 'Technically durable' are the words Bergman used to describe him. The same applies to Gunnar Björnstrand in the role of the pastor, unwell at the time of filming and under Bergman's direction giving off an air of suppressed emotion that manages to lend conviction to an extremely difficult character, a pastor who has come up against the silence of God. The temporal tightness of the film, since the action takes place over a period of less than 12 hours, and the spatial constrictions, since it unfolds in two adjacent rural parishes, allow Bergman to show Ericsson in those key relationships. First Jonas Persson comes for advice after the morning

Eucharist. Oppressed by fear of nuclear destruction, he seeks a reason for living but the pastor can only talk about himself and the way he had encountered God's silence. Persson leaves and commits suicide (shades of Dr Delbende in *Journal*). Then Märta, the schoolteacher, in love with Ericsson, follows him around fussing over him, until sitting in the schoolroom they confront each other, Ericsson baldly stating he does not want her, she countering that he will die of hatred. In the parish of Frostnäs, as he prepares for evensong, the parish clerk expounds his view of the passion, that Jesus suffered in three ways: physically on the cross, secondly in knowing that the disciples did not understand his words or the meaning of his passion, and thirdly and most devastatingly, in the glimpse on the cross of God's silence: 'Why hast thou forsaken me?'

The exposition of the parish clerk is heavily ironic, pouring out his own reasons for unbelief to a person who earlier in the film had grossly failed Jonas Persson. In that encounter, Ericsson is triggered into analysing his own version of God's silence and sketches a vision of a world without God: death will be mere extinction and people's cruelty and suffering are simply self-evident facts of nature requiring no theological explanation; there is no immeasurable Creator 'to make one's head spin'. Confronted with the arguments for atheism rather than the message of hope that his wife hoped the pastor would give, Persson, completely cornered, takes the logical way out from his agony by committing suicide.

All three of the pastor's relationships explored in the film, with Persson, with Märta and with the parish clerk, embody the silence of God which the pastor is experiencing. Yet there is a fourth key relationship, which suggests something of the grace he has lost: he still mourns for his dead wife. One senses the presence of Sartre ('Hell is other people') and it is only the person who has left his life that the pastor longs for. The film is essentially a study of loneliness and the absence of faith it analyses is the incapacity of the pastor to love anyone living. Its quality lies in the analysis. Just as we see Märta in a flashback rip off the bandages from her hands to reveal the eczema she suffers from, Bergman rips the metaphysical bandages from these people to show the starkness of their mental torment. The actors' faces convey tightness and suppressed hysteria; the dialogue largely dispenses with the niceties of conversation as if they were irrelevant banalities to the only fit subject of discussion, namely the existence of God, while the camera is square on to the characters, filming in medium shot and close-up, with the winter light diffused across these drained faces, a sort of revelling in the grey scale.

Bergman's roots were in the theatre and although he both wrote and directed a large number of films, he also spent much of his time as a theatre director and from 1963 to 1966 was even head of the Royal Dramatic Theatre in Stockholm. His films often observe theatrical forms. For example *Winter Light* is essentially in five acts: the communion and after-communion in the parish church, the site of Persson's suicide, the confrontation with Märta in the schoolhouse, the visit to Persson's widow, the evening service at Frostnäs. The script itself is theatrical: the words are spoken with dramatic emphasis and their content is like a play's, since, with only 80 minutes to tell the story, they quickly move from superficial conversation to intense matter.

Bergman is an inheritor of Strindberg and the psychological chamber drama that strips its protagonists bare. One of the reasons for the fascination which Bergman exercised for audiences was the sense they had of human vulnerability being exposed, that Bergman for all his atmosphere of lovelessness, was ultimately compassionate. In *Winter Light* Bergman chooses to end in ambiguity as if at the end there is something to cling onto. Despite the pastor's pastoral failings, his life continues. Märta, following her rejection at Ericsson's hands, does not hesitate to offer to drive him to Frostnäs for evensong. Since she, the organist and the parish clerk are the sum total of the congregation, the question is put to the pastor whether the service should be cancelled. The deeper question is unspoken: if God will not communicate with him, what is the point of an act of worship? Ericsson goes ahead and thus speaks the last words of the film before the altar: 'Holy, holy, holy is Lord God Almighty, the whole earth is full of his glory.'

The end makes an intriguing contrast with *Journal*. The last words of both book and film are 'What does it matter? All is grace' and the film shows the shadow of the cross on a wall as if it was the earthly imprint of the young priest's departed soul. Out of the ruins of human relationships, Bresson finds triumph. Bergman on the other hand inverts the elements. While Bresson balances death with salvation and the male priest burns those who come near him, Bergman chooses a woman, Märta, who strives to use her fire to melt the male iciness of the pastor. He juxtaposes the message of glory with dreariness, he closes on the pastor's empty visage reciting the liturgy without conviction. There is a larger contrast too: in *Journal* the Catholic doctrine of salvation and the operation of divine grace mean that the priest's night of doubt is overcome by his persistence in his voca-tion, Mother Church being larger than the individual. In *Winter Light* on the other hand the Lutheran emphasis on personal meaning has the result that, where no such meaning is found, the vocation looks profoundly suspect and the church edifice begins to crumble.

It is particularly significant that these two stories of crisis – the priest of *Journal* wrestling with the litany of sin, Pastor Ericsson wrestling with silence – take place in a rural setting. As dramas, they achieve a heightened quality by being set in a claustropho-bic world. Emotional relationships in small communities become magnified, on a cosmic scale almost. The tradition of the rural parish priest throughout Christendom poses particular strains on the human ability to communicate with each other, to love and to hate, to conquer sin and suffering. Each story in its own way testifies to the central question of how humans reveal their love for each other.

Another film about a priest, *Sous le soleil de Satan*, sends us back again to Georges Bernanos. *Journal d'un curé de campagne*, published in 1936 to become his most celebrated novel, is a culmination of his preoccupation with defining the nature of priesthood. This had begun with *Sous le soleil de Satan* (*Under Satan's Sun*), written in the mid-1920s in cafés and station buffets when Bernanos worked for an insurance company. This method of composition may account for its disjointed quality since it is in three distinct sections. The last part was written first and depicts an elderly rural priest, Father Donissan, in the tiny hamlet of Lumbres where he has achieved sainthood on earth. The central incident is his raising of a dead child back to life, following which he has an attack of angina and dies. The first part of the novel, which was written second, is the story of sixteen-year-old Germaine Malorthy, pregnant seemingly by the Marquis de Cadignan. Coming to his house late one night, she asks to be taken away from her family to Paris but finds no comfort. In the morning, she shoots him with a shot-gun but the inquest pronounces it to be suicide. She visits another of her lovers, Dr Gallet, the doctor and government *deputé* for the area, which ends with her in hysterics: she is taken to a nursing home and a month later gives birth to a stillborn child. The middle and longest part titled 'The Temptation of Despair', which was written last, tells of Donissan as a young priest, under the pastoral guidance of Canon Menou-Segrais, dean of the parish of Campagne in northern France. The dean, a well-born, experienced and comfortable priest, having battled with secular authority, has the air of disappointed hopes about him, in contrast to Donissan who is of peasant stock, self-critical and uncertain of his vocation. Despite the contrast, Bernanos gives them an affinity: Donissan respects Menou-Segrais' guidance, while the dean sees the germ of saintliness in the young priest (as Torcy does with the priest of *Journal*).

The crisis in the second part of the novel revolves round an encounter Donissan has with an itinerant horse-dealer in the open countryside. He is lost when the horse-dealer appears to bring help but turns out to be Satan in disguise. Donissan feels a miracle occurs: he sees into his antagonist's soul for what he is. When he awakes the next morning he returns to Campagne but meets Germaine Malorthy on the way and thanks to his inner vision proceeds to reveal to her the details not only of her life and family, but also of the killing of the Marquis, confronting her as a victim of Satan. She flees from him. The section ends in gross melodrama: when she returns home, she cuts her throat. Donissan rushes to the house where in her death throes she declares a wish to be taken to the church to die. Donissan snatches the body from her father's hands and carries her to the foot of the altar. In the aftermath, his superiors criticise the dean for letting it happen and having condemned Donissan for 'excesses (which) belong to another age', send him to the Trappist monastery at Tortefontaine to be cured. Five years later he is appointed to the hamlet of Lumbres to become a 'new curé d'Ars', the nineteenth-century priest who attracted large numbers of pilgrims to his confessional in the tiny village of Ars.

Like *Diary of a Country Priest*, the story does not seem especially promising as a film, yet 60 years after its publication the distinguished French film-maker, Maurice Pialat, decided to turn it into one, perhaps in recognition of the continued interest in Bernanos as a writer, at least in France. It is hardly conceivable that in doing so he was unaware of or indifferent to Bresson's version of *Journal* and the result can be read as a critique not just of Bernanos' Catholicism, for he focuses on the ambiguities inherent in *Sous le soleil de Satan,* but also of Bresson's style in that he seeks to reassert the values of professional acting, casting the noted French star Gérard Depardieu as Donissan, and as Germaine the young Sandrine Bonnaire (but being nineteen years old, not as young as the girl she plays) whom Pialat had made into a star in two previous films. He himself took the role of Menou-Segrais, the dean.

Bresson's *Journal* has a particular place in film history as marking the true starting-point of the Bressonian style: using what he calls 'models' and not actors to play the roles, he strips away the physical representation of emotion in the way words are spoken and gestures performed in order to achieve a sort of tonelessness. His 'models' thus deliver an inner performance

that Bresson regarded as spiritual. At the same time he reduces
the surroundings to a just visible background ('Don't let your
backgrounds absorb the faces you are applying to them' he
wrote) so that the story has a recognisable setting but the camera
is fixed wholly on the relation between people. For the curé of
Journal he chose a young believer called Claude Laydu who bears
in the film traces of inner agony, just as Bresson wished.

Pialat's tactics are very different. He reduces background less
than Bresson and his approach to film direction, like Ingmar
Bergman's, is theatrical. Scenes are worked out with the actor,
with the camera placed to observe performance. Emphasis is
thrown onto the dialogue, hence slowing the action down. In
writing the screenplay of *Journal*, Bresson uses short scenes to
concentrate on the story, skilfully distilling long speeches in
Bernanos' novel. The exception to this is the pivotal scene
between the Countess and the curé where the Bressonian
method comes under particular strain since the actors' tonelessness is at constant odds with the drama of the dialogue. The
scene lasts nine minutes and demands the spectator's concentration. Only at the end when the Countess kneels to be
blessed does Bresson use Grünenwald's music to underline the
resolution of the conflict.

In *Under Satan's Sun* Pialat by contrast does not hesitate to
reflect the big conversations with big performances – between
Menou-Segrais and Donissan, between Germaine and the
Marquis and then Dr Gallet, between Donissan and the horse-
dealer. As it turns out, this contest between the two styles does
not necessarily produce a winner. Bernanos' two novels could be
criticised for melodramatic excess, especially in the portrayal of
the two priests, both willing themselves to death in the conduct
of their ministry. But the novels do not aim to portray the literal-
ness of the people and of their lives, rather to reveal the
metaphors they carry: priests are the shock troops in a cosmic
battle with human viciousness and enter the fray bearing the
weight of universal sin and anguish. In the novel of *Under Satan's
Sun*, when Donissan reveals to Germaine all her history, he

spreads it to relations and ancestors, peeling back outward irre-
proachability to tell of 'major misdeeds', of her flesh 'marked
and weakened by all those sins from the moment of her conception'. When he came to write *Diary of a Country Priest*,
Bernanos makes the idea literal: the priest has to do battle with
the alcoholism which has infected his family blood from way
back and which can only be redeemed as the blood of the sacrament. While Bresson's austere style produces an aura of profound seriousness, the conservatism of Pialat's style does no
disservice to this cosmic struggle. Bonnaire mixes assertion and
fragility; Depardieu's large frame and lost looks are pitted against
the smiling horse-dealer, torturing Donnissan as he smiles;
Donissan's callowness spars with Menou-Segrais' bearded wisdom.
Pialat manages to suppress the hysteria, so that when it does
burst forth in Germaine's screams or in Donissan lifting the dead
child and calling on some supernatural power to show who is
master, real tension is created. The film only falls apart when
Pialat shows Donissan laying the blood-stained body of
Germaine at the foot of the altar: his mouth is smeared in blood,
Germaine's mother embraces the corpse, Germaine's father
assaults the dean. Whereas in the novel Bernanos cleverly
reports the scene in a clinical letter from Donissan's Bishop to a
colleague so that the melodrama, recounted at one remove,
becomes detached, the film gives us Grand Guignol, the camera
falling prey to the temptation to show everything.

Pialat's theatricality is also the source of a major difference
between novel and film, which helps him to underline the ambiguity of the story. Instead of accepting the structure of Bernanos'
three distinct sections (Mouchette's Story/The Temptation of
Despair/The Saint of Lumbres) spread over a long period, he con-
tracts the time and indeed space into a single unity: Germaine's
and Donissan's stories are told in parallel rather than in
sequence so they are interwoven and Donissan is still a young
man when he has achieved his sainthood and resurrects the
dead child. He marks the stages of the story with the use of a
highly arresting fragment from Henri Dutilleux's First

Symphony, starting with soft but sombre cellos and then overlaid by tense violins: for the opening credits (Act 1); for the start of Donissan's cross-country journey (Act 2); when he takes leave of the dean to go to the monastery and thence to Lumbres (Act 3); and again for the final crisis when Donissan returns from the farmhouse where the sick child has lain and succumbs to the stroke leading to his death.

Pialat also changes the end in a vital way: the book reaches its climax when a member of the Académie Française, Antoine Saint-Marin, visits Lumbres to meet the priest for the vaguest of motives, which appear to include the garnering of ideas for a new book. It is Saint-Marin who finds Donissan dead in the confessional, whose 'whole body seemed to be miming a dreadful challenge: "You wanted my peace! Come and take it!"'. The scene constitutes a full-frontal assault by Bernanos on that bastion of cultural authority, the Académie Française, aiming to blast it to ruins by the spiritual power of Donissan's death.

Pialat matches this final twist but there is no Academician present. Instead it is the dean, who on a visit to see his former protégé and wandering through the church to look for him opens the door of the confessional to reveal Donissan's body. His ghostly face is like a death mask. The dean wearily walks back down the church, past a cross on the far wall. The film ends again with the death's head and repeats Dutilleux's fragment, still musically unresolved.

Indeed, ambiguity is at the heart of Pialat's version. Whereas Bernanos' impassioned Catholicism, in revolt against comfort and republicanism, sought to redefine the nature of priesthood, Pialat is more taken with the outward specifics of the story. There is a vivid episode in the novel where Donissan mortifies his body by whipping himself repeatedly with a chain. Pialat, and seemingly Depardieu as well, relish the inclusion of this scene in the film. Yet, in the novel, it is prompted by an encounter with an invisible other, while in the film we only witness with revulsion a man privately scourging himself. In the novel, Germaine's self-mutilation with her father's razor is done in a conscious wish for deliverance: she asks Donissan to take her to the church to die. This is quite excluded from the film: we see only a troubled girl and the mechanics of suicide. On the other hand, in both novel and film, the meeting with the trick-ster horse-dealer is as if Donissan were looking in the mirror. At the start of this sequence, Donissan, hopelessly lost, is seen wan-dering aimlessly over vast wintry fields in the folds of downland. The horse-dealer falls in with him, and when Donissan stumbles to the ground in weariness, embraces and kisses him. He ends by offering Donissan a boon or grace, namely to see into human souls, and Donissan is unable to resist. One immediate result is Germaine's self-destruction. Furthermore, when near the end he visits the Havret farmhouse and lifts the lifeless body of the child into the air shouting 'show me who is master' even though the boy then opens his eyes it remains unclear whether this resur-rection is the work of God, or of a Devil provoking Donissan to remember his supernatural power. When the boy awakes and Donissan, dropping the body, rocks backwards, the mother shrieks 'he's alive' in hysteria – like those of Germaine, her screams are more diabolical than divine. When Donissan had recounted the miracle of his meeting with first the horse-dealer then Germaine, the dean commented, 'the sign is equivocal'. By the end, Donissan comments to a fellow priest, 'Satan is prince of this world.'

This equivocation is a measure of Bernanos' encounter with doubt and despair. He rejects the fixed comforts of nineteenth-century Catholicism, aware of a new and emerging conflict between the faithful and the non-believer, bringing to his writ-ing a blistering candour. Night is more than just the absence of light, but the presence of spiritual darkness, the moment when Donissan meets Satan, or when the young priest in *Journal* ex-periences the catastrophe of despair. It is the time when the celibate male is alone with his body, prey to his imagination. It is the time when the order constructed during the day is under-mined and thrown down. Furthermore, Bernanos' sympathy for his male celibates is matched by a distrust of females: Germaine and Chantal are two of a kind, young, attractive and poisonous. This distrust Bernanos boldly extends to the family, the place of outwardly irreproachable lives where wealth is accumulated and beneath whose veneer is resentment and hatred.

To balance this cruel conception of the world and of people, Bernanos gives his priestly heroes a quality of incandescence, the capacity to burn all who come near them. He can even find something of the same quality in his female characters. Chantal and Germaine have the same fire, and the novels and the films are about the sublimation of that fire in judgement and salvation.

3

Faith

In the prison of his days,
Teach the free man how to praise.
W. H. Auden, 'In Memory of W. B. Yeats'

Bresson's, Bergman's and Pialat's priests are all created in response to a crisis of faith in the West, articulating a new uncertainty in the way we perceive the Church, repository of eternal values. There is therefore a certain irony in the fact that the film-maker who turned out to be a remarkable advocate of the certain need for faith came out of the brutal experiment with atheism conducted in the Soviet Union. Born after the Revolution of 1917, Andrei Tarkovsky might have emerged as a pure product of 'scientific atheism', the new Soviet man free of obscurantism and confident in the achievements of Communism. The opposite is the case. Tarkovsky's heroes are seekers of meaning who find it in innocent faith, in reconciliation, in sacrifice, even in holy foolishness. Their stories are ones of pilgrimage: they are engaged in a mental journey and usually a physical one as well, through the chaos or the spiritual emptiness around them until they find a point where faith can be asserted and a resolution found.

In *Nostalgia* he depicts his hero Andrei Gorchakov in the abbey of San Galgano in Tuscany. The camera starts in the north

aisle and tracks across rather than down the abbey, moving from
north aisle to nave, where it picks up Gorchakov walking aimlessly and follows him to the south aisle. Coming to a rest, the
camera shows him gazing upwards and then turning and walking away. The scene is an arresting one because the abbey is a
ruined Cistercian building, the abbot having sold off the lead in
the sixteenth century with the result that the roof finally col-
lapsed in 1786. Since then, it has stood open to the elements and
the floors are now earth and grass. But this setting, which is what
strikes the viewer at first, is only half the picture. As we gaze at
Gorchakov, we eavesdrop on a conversation on the soundtrack:

> A (*female voice*): Lord, don't you see how he's asking? Say
>   something to him.
> B (*male voice*): But what would happen if he heard my voice?
> A: Let him feel your presence.
> B: I always do, but he's not aware of it.

Gorchakov is a writer in Italy, researching a Russian composer
who had lived there in the eighteenth century. Like his subject,
and indeed like the director of the film, he suffers from an
intense longing to return to Russia, hence the film's title,
Nostalgia, not used in the pallid sense common now but in the
Homeric sense of Odysseus' longing (*nostos*) to return to the
homeland, a feeling that can produce not just melancholy but
despair. Tarkovsky even went so far as to define it as 'a global
yearning for the whole of existence'. Gorchakov is in fact his
double and the film an analysis of the dislocation Tarkovsky
experienced personally in being separated from Russia and his
family after 1982. But in this particular scene, he charges the
feeling of nostalgia with a spiritual electricity, since the two
voices on the soundtrack are none other than those of one of
God's angels and of God himself.

The cultural undercurrents of the film and the way they reflect
on its maker are especially intriguing. Tarkovsky is Russian but
he is also Soviet Russian: born in 1932, a boy through the darkest days of Stalinism, twelve at the time of the Soviet Union's

great victory over Nazi Germany in 1945, spending his formative years during Soviet Communism's period of stability before the forces of implosion began seriously to take hold, and dying in 1986, just as *perestroika* was beginning to dissolve the Soviet Union. He was a natural dissident, with a sure conviction of his vocation, not just as a film-maker but also as an artist in the Russian tradition, holding that there was no more important human enterprise on earth than the artistic one. But his dissidence is displayed to no greater effect than his clinging to the centrality of religious belief against not just the Marxist-Leninist tide but also the fashionable intellectual West. His films are utterly without irony. He viewed the making of great art as meeting a spiritual need – an ethical project central to the development of society, an endeavour to explain the meaning of existence. Like religion, which is rooted in an intuition about the world which leads to faith, art is a 'kind of detector of infinity' (as he wrote in his artistic credo, *Sculpting in Time*). In his diaries from 1970 to 1986, Tarkovsky notes his interest in a wide range of spiritual thinkers and ideas: parapsychology, Rudolph Steiner's theosophy, Radha-Krishnan, Castañeda, transcendental meditation, yoga, Buddhism, Gurdjiev. But the bedrock to this interest in the spiritual appears to be the Christian faith. One remarkable sequence in his *Andrei Rublev* enacts the crucifixion in a snowy landscape and in the same film he quotes the passage about love from Paul's first letter to the Corinthians. His favourite piece of music was Bach's *St John Passion*.

Tarkovsky's first full-length film, *Ivan's Childhood* (1962), brought him to international notice when it won the Golden Lion at the Venice Film Festival, but it was the making of his next film, *Andrei Rublev* (1966) that brought him fame. Not that this happened instantly. The film is over three hours long and was three years in the making. Although they had allowed it to be made in the first place, it was then banned from public view by the Soviet authorities for five years. It did not reach the West until 1972, yet because news seeped out of this extraordinary film, which the Soviets had tried to suppress, its reputation had preceded it. When it was put on show, both in the Soviet Union and in the West, its impact was remarkable. While on first viewing, many people find Tarkovsky's other films slow and impenetrable, *Rublev* remains approachable and overwhelming. Nor is the story of its making ended because in the past few years a longer version has appeared, adding 39 minutes to the first, enhancing its epic quality and revealing more closely Tarkovsky's original intentions over which he had to compromise. Finally, a version, reputedly some four hours long, was shown in Moscow in 1988.

Although Tarkovsky is the prophet of faith, he could hardly have been more the victim of doubt. *Rublev* is a parable of faith overcoming chaos but for much of its huge length, doubt and confusion hold the upper hand. It starts in 1400 and ends in 1423. At the beginning, Rublev is one of three monks who shelter from the rain in a hut crowded with peasants being entertained by a jester. The scene ends when the latter is brutally arrested by soldiers. One of the monks is Kirill who meets with the icon-painter Theophanes the Greek and remarks of Rublev that he has 'no awe, no faith' and this is undermining his art. This section is a pair with the following one entitled 'The Passion According to Andrei (1406)'. In it, Rublev meets Theophanes, who argues as Dostoevsky's Grand Inquisitor in *The Brothers Karamazov* had done, that if Jesus were to return to earth he would be crucified again. This is followed by the vision of the crucifixion at Calvary being re-enacted in the snow. In the next section Rublev on his travels is drawn into witnessing pagan rites on St John's Night and is tempted by a woman. This moment of faithlessness leads into section five showing him at work in a pristine monastery seeking to find a way of painting the walls. But inspiration has deserted him and Rublev is too paralysed to begin. Section six is set in 1408, as the previous two had been, and the three comprise a trio: distraction by temptation (section four), alienation by loss of inspiration (section five) and destruction by devastation (section six): this sixth section depicts, in the second longest sequence in the film, the sacking of the Russian town of Vladimir by invading Tartars amidst scenes of confusion, terror and cruelty. Rublev is caught in the thick of it and in rescuing a woman from an attacker, he kills him. Shocked by this act of violence, he makes a vow neither to paint nor even to speak. Section seven, entitled 'The Silence (1412)' shows Rublev's nadir. The land is paralysed by famine and occupied by the Tartars. Rublev returns with the woman he has rescued to the monastery and finds the monks there, like himself, utterly dispirited. When the invaders take off the woman he has saved, he is unable to prevent them. The scene is set for the climax of the film.

To bring Rublev's story to a conclusion, Tarkovsky jumps eleven years to 1423 and daringly switches the focus of the last section to showing how a young boy, Boris, casts a new bell for the Grand Prince. Boris' father had been a bell-maker but had died in the plague. When the prince's men come looking for him, Boris (or rather Boriska, as he comes to be called) argues with them that with his father and the community dead: 'there's no one left to cast the bell, take me. I know the secret from father.' Initially reluctant, they do so in the absence of any alternative. Boriska then proceeds to cast a giant bell which involves locating a suitable hillock in which to dig a large hole, finding the right clay, melting down a huge quantity of metal, removing the clay to reveal the bell, lifting it by a scaffold, ropes and an army of helpers and then testing the bell in front of the Grand Prince. This bare account barely hints at the massiveness of the undertaking: the boy has to overcome the scepticism of his team of workmen but once he has done so, the project grows to embrace all the townspeople. Boriska achieves his task as a result of complete self-confidence: for example, short of metal for the casting, he orders the prince's men to give him another 18 pounds of silver. Only as the moment approaches when the bell must be rung to ensure it sounds true does he shrink from completing the task, the enormity of it only dawning on him at the end: failure to make a 'true' bell would mean the execution of him and his fellow workers.

The episode generates a wonderful suspense: when the clapper is swung back and forth until finally it makes an arc long enough to strike the bell, a rich sound breaks over the silence and the relief of success is accompanied by an explosion of joy in the crowd. The twist in the tale is that Boriska had not inherited the secret of bell casting from his father who it turns out had refused to tell him before he died. Boriska's success is based on half-knowledge and intuition.

The film does not however end with Boriska but with Rublev. As the bell-making gets under way, Rublev turns up and, fascinated by the proceedings, stays as an observer. Boriska's completion of the task is enough to shake Rublev from his vow of silence and his refusal to paint. After Boriska confesses to him that he did not after all know the secret, Rublev breaks into speech again, telling him that they will work together, 'you casting bells, I painting icons'. Drawing inspiration from the young boy's innocent faith in his power to succeed, Rublev lays aside his deep inhibition. In a *coup de cinéma* the film moves from black and white to colour and ends in a blaze of icons while Ovchinnikov's choral music strives to prolong the moment of resolution, to celebrate Rublev's flowering. The very last image is of four horses grazing by a river in the rain.

Ostensibly, the film is about artistic achievement and, like *Nostalgia*, has a strong autobiographical element. Rublev and Boris are both aspects of Tarkovsky, the former his doubtful self, struggling in the spiritual desert of Soviet society to give expression to his inner world, the latter his innocent self who, thirty-two years old and on only his second feature, undertakes a film which like the bell is made on a massive scale and triumphs at the end.

The creating of the bell has a documentary feel; it is as if Tarkovsky got his cast to carry out in real life the making of a bell while he filmed it so that the army of helpers involved will have reflected the conditions of the production. Several shots are long sweeping camera tracks and cranes in order to do justice to the communal efforts involved. The seething activity in front of the camera will have been matched by that behind it.

What motivated Tarkovsky to undertake such a project? *Andrei Rublev* gives an answer: faith – in oneself. His book of essays on the cinema, *Sculpting in Time*, repeats the message. In writing about the reaction to *Mirror* and his belief that the audience would put aside their initial incomprehension and come to see its qualities, Tarkovsky wrote: 'In the end we were saved by one thing only – faith: the belief that since our work was so important to us it would not but become equally important to the audience.'

Tarkovsky has an exalted view of the artist as articulating the most intimate and vital truths about the meaning of human existence. When in his diary in 1977 he had written, 'A person has no need of society, it is society that needs him,' he means that it is creative individuals who shape and lead society, not social structures and organisations. In *Sculpting in Time* he accuses the Church of caricaturing social institutions: '. . . the Church shows no sign of being able to redress the balance with a call to a spiritual awakening'. Hence 'art is called to express the absolute freedom of man's spiritual position': the camera is mightier than the cope.

This confidence in the artistic process explains the seriousness with which Tarkovsky approached his film-making. When he died, he had only seven full-length films to his credit, spread over 25 years. This paucity of finished work derives in part from the obstructions put in his way by the authorities but there is a deeper reason. His obsessive, perfectionist approach meant that projects went through several versions before they were completed and are all the better for going through this refining process. Secondly, the conviction that his films should reveal his innermost thoughts and concerns means that, despite their disparate subject matter – war film, historical epic, science fiction, autobiography, modern drama – there is a remarkable unity to the corpus. The most notable example is a recurrent fascination with water, especially (but not only) still water. The flooded winter landscape of *Ivan's Childhood*, the rain in *Rublev*, the image of the waving weeds in the stream that opens *Solaris*, the dream in *Mirror* of his mother washing her hair in a tub, the flooded wasteland of *Stalker*, the drowned house in *Nostalgia* and Little Man in *The Sacrifice* watering the barren tree until it sprouts. Tarkovsky's images are not I think intended to be symbolic, but, for example, by its rhythm and by the sense of the eternal it conveys, the image of horses in the pouring rain which closes *Andrei Rublev* is meant to convey a sense of completion and fulfilment.

Another idea to fascinate him was how we might bring into existence our innermost thoughts and desires. It is first encountered in the science fiction *Solaris*: Kris travels to the space station to find the astronauts troubled by the influence of the planet Solaris which they have been sent to study. It has the power to bring to life the observer's subconscious with the result that Kris, obsessed with the loss of his wife Hari, soon finds her materialising before him and then decaying, a false resurrection. In *Nostalgia*, Gorchakov's girlfriend visits a church to see Piero della Francesca's *Madonna of Childbirth* where she discovers that women make the pilgrimage to see it in order to realise their wishes for a child. That the wish expressed in prayer can be brought to fulfilment then becomes the hinge of the drama in *Nostalgia* and *The Sacrifice*. In his diary in 1970, Tarkovsky had written: 'Thank God for people who burn themselves alive in front of an impassive, wordless crowd.' This idea is realised in *Nostalgia* where Domenico burns himself to death in the Piazza del Campidoglio in Rome in order to save mankind, while *The Sacrifice* is the story of Alexander who, on the threshold of nuclear catastrophe, prays to God that he might avert it if he sacrifices all the comforts of the world – home, possessions, links with his family.

Domenico and Alexander, like Boriska in *Rublev*, take the giant step out of this material world into the unknown, in order to release some innermost essence in human beings for love and creativity. For us as audience things only exist when we see them; when we do not see them, they do not exist. For Tarkovsky as creator, art can make visible things we had not seen, can raise into existence a supposedly invisible world. In this he belongs emphatically to the twentieth century when the new science of psychology was added to the traditional ones and when the new art of cinema joined the historical Muses. As new-comers, film and psychology feel an instant attraction, for when combined they bring to light the unmentionable, the ineffable, the unthinkable, the unimaginable. Led by them, stumbling into daylight after centuries of imprisonment in the human mind, have come images of the horrid and the terrifying, the obscene and the erotic, the weird and the extraordinary. Only the cinema has the necessary artifice to represent this new reality, overlaying the world with a tissue of dreams and nightmares.

Yet the seeming boundlessness of the human imagination still finds human action imprisoned. Take a film in which the char-acters construct a barrier invisible to the spectator that roots them to the spot, prevents them getting food and drink, turns their claustrophobia to thoughts of murder. Such is the premise of Luis Buñuel's *The Exterminating Angel*: a group of about 20 people retire to the music room after their main meal, listen to a piano recital, then feel that it is time to go – but cannot bring themselves to leave the room. Instead they lie down to sleep, but the next day is no better, nor the day after that . . . For the spec-tator there is no barrier visible; for the actors in their roles, an obstacle they cannot see but cannot cross pens them in.

It is an interesting speculation that among the films Tarkovsky saw in Moscow in the early 1960s, in the window of the Khrushchev thaw, was *The Exterminating Angel*. Buñuel is among the handful of film directors he put in his pantheon in *Sculpting in Time* (along with Bresson, Bergman, Kurosawa, Mizoguchi, Antonioni, Fellini, Vigo and Dovzhenko). Did the idea lodge in his mind then as a fruitful cinematic device? Buñuel's allegory is about the monumental inadequacy of human relations: life is spiteful, malicious, vicious; desires struggle to be fulfilled and fail. Buñuel is certainly the central figure in The Filmgoer's Guide to Godlessness. He rejoices in paradox: an absurd situation is made believable by cinema; the miraculous imagination of the film-maker is used to depict the human failure to take imaginative action. Everywhere we erect our own prison walls.

If Tarkovsky *had* seen *The Exterminating Angel*, when he comes to take up the idea he makes something different: his cinematic imagination creates a forbidden zone; after entering it illegally, three men make their way to its centre. They are surrounded by nature but it is not paradise. Their journey is through derelict buildings overwhelmed by growth, sinking in mud and water. At the centre of this Zone is a decaying industrial building and at the centre of the building is a Room where the most cherished dreams come true, not our surface desires but the deep-down ones, maybe for universal peace or universal chaos, for spiritual peace or spiritual power, for an encounter with the divine or the diabolical. This Room is first described verbally to the spectator; second, when the three men are on its threshold it is imagined off-screen by the spectator; finally, when it comes to the close encounter, it is revealed to the spectator as a void, a large brick-lined space whose floor is a pool of water, from whose ceiling natural light filters down. As in the Buñuel film, the three are unable to bring themselves to go in.

This scene is the climax of *Stalker*. To link Tarkovsky with Buñuel is to take two poles, the one of affirming, the other of rejecting God as an ultimately fruitful goal for human seeking. For both life is mired in suffering: for Buñuel that there is no exit is a tragedy, for Tarkovsky the exit is only reached through the need for deep change in human beings. Buñuel's world-view is a cul-de-sac, Tarkovsky's a route to fulfilment. Watching *Stalker* is like being in a cathedral: like Gorchakov in San Galgano, you wanted to come but were not sure why, now you are here its splendour is overwhelming, but where is its heart? Where is it leading? And when you are close to what you came for, do you recognise it? And when you recognise it, can you make it your own? Can you bring to fruition your most cherished desire?

The leader of the group of three men is the Stalker, honoured in the title of the film. He makes his living by taking paying customers into the Zone past guarded checkpoints at risk to life but once he is inside, the guards are too frightened to pursue. The Stalker is an individual who ekes out an existence at the margins, a social dissident, the last who in fact may be first. The two accompanying him are portentously named Writer and Scientist, that is to say representatives of two classes with privileged status in twentieth-century society, having usurped some of the Church's power to influence and determine what humans should think and do.

Despite their portrayal as worldly and world-weary, Tarkovsky is anxious to show that there is still some inmost part of them that is not satisfied: having concluded that literary success and making scientific discoveries have a limit to their value, they want to go into the Zone, to find the Room, to see this great thing of which they have heard. But having got there, the Writer will not go in, and pours scorn on the humiliation of praying, while the Scientist produces a bomb with which he contemplates blowing up the Room on the grounds that it cannot bring anyone any hope. When the distraught Stalker fights with the Scientist over the bomb, the Writer prevents the Stalker. The Scientist then accuses the Writer of being a hypocrite, the Writer turns on the Stalker for not going into the Room himself and accuses him of being a parasite on the two pilgrims, seeking only to exercise power over them until the Stalker tearfully explains he is not allowed to enter the Room. At this the recriminations subside: when the Writer almost topples into the Room by accident, the Stalker stops him; the Writer wears an air of contrition; the Scientist dismantles his bomb, renders it ineffectual and throws away the different parts. Tarkovsky then makes a major cut from action to transcendental stasis: the camera switches to a view of the Room giving the spectator a first sight of this spiritual space. At the far end, the three men sit down on the threshold and gaze into it and the Stalker wistfully imagines coming to lie there with his wife and child.

Ostensibly *Stalker* works both as filmed theatre and as cinema, and one of the creative tensions in watching it is for the spectator to resolve which is the more important. It is theatrical because of the bravura performance by the three actors, Kaidanovsky, Solonitsyn and Grinko, using all their skill with gesture and voice to embody Tarkovsky's pilgrims. It is theatrical too because of the density of the script, Tarkovsky's most explicit meditation on the religio-philosophical themes that obsessed him. For a moment one can be seduced into imagining the drama finding its essence in a theatre where both actor and spectator can both concentrate without distraction on the words of the message. But Tarkovsky is a film-maker who reserves his most intense moments for image and sound combined. This means that there are two ways of experiencing the scene at the Room. The first is to try and follow the conflicts between the three men's view of the world as it is expressed in words, only to conclude that the motivation is obscure (for example, why does the Writer stop Stalker from wresting the bomb from the Scientist?) and their situation artificial. The second is to absorb all the verbal sparring but to balance it with what Tarkovsky does with his camera, that is to say to capture the shifting relationships of the three men by its movements and their movements, to use close-ups on faces to reveal their experience, their suffering, their humanity, and then to crown the scene with something virtuosic: a shot lasting seven minutes, beginning in apparent banality – a view of an ugly and depressing space – and ending in the profound stillness of reconciliation, of light falling on water, on the sound of single water drops echoing in space, and maybe of drawing the spectator to a moment of prayer for his or her most cherished desire.

Tarkovsky was very drawn to miracles and wonders: the dead boy soldier, Ivan, playing on some sunlit shore (*Ivan's Childhood*), the medieval peasant on a balloon flight (*Andrei Rublev*), Hari's resurrection (*Solaris*), a blazing barn in the forest

(*Mirror*), Gorchakov carrying the lit candle the length of St Catherine's pool at Bagno Vignoni as the final healing of his troubled mind (*Nostalgia*), a levitating witch (*The Sacrifice*). The miracle of *Stalker* is more hidden. When Parsifal first witnesses the ceremony of Holy Communion in Wagner's opera of that name, he is at first baffled by the sight, so no miracle occurs. Similarly with the Writer and Scientist on the threshold of the Room: no miracle. But Tarkovsky is showing us that they are witnesses at some eucharistic moment, when, once the miracle of faith is achieved, they can realise their deepest desire, find their innermost being.

While the single shot of the Room is the climax, it is not the end. Tarkovsky adds a remarkable coda. He cuts from the Room to a scene of the Stalker with his two travellers, plus the dog who joined them on the journey, back outside the Zone from which they started. His wife and child come to collect him. The three return to their home where the Stalker, overcome by despair, lies on the floor crying, 'They don't believe in anything. Their capacity for faith has atrophied through lack of use.' His wife tries to calm him and puts him to bed. Then she goes to the corner of the room and delivers a monologue direct to the camera, i.e. to the spectator, explaining why she became his wife: that he's one of God's fools but she's never regretted marrying him. It brought grief, fear and pain, but this is 'just fate, life, it's us. Without sorrow there is no happiness, without happiness there is no hope.'

4

Salvation by Water

Deep river, my home is over Jordan,
I want to cross over into campground, Lord.
Spiritual

Russian suffering can be overcome by faith in God the Father, the centuries-old God who beyond all pain and despair heals mankind. In the United States of America, a more instant version of salvation is to be found. Some 29 million Americans are Baptists, whose numbers underestimate their importance to the formation of American values, for they have contributed some defining characteristics to America as a nation: missionary zeal, moral uprightness and 'self-madeness'. Anyone can be a Baptist leader if they have enough drive in them to form and lead a community.

The Baptist church is particularly concentrated in the rural South, making up for poverty of living with an abundance of spirit. This latter point is important to understanding its appeal: a simple black and white moral code is necessary to deal with the rigours of poverty and instant salvation can give an escape from the daily grind, a religious version of winning a lottery. Baptist and revivalist culture is therefore prey to the contempt of liberal, educated film-makers, two examples of unsympathetic treatment being *Elmer Gantry* and *The Neon Bible*. Richard

Brooks' film of *Elmer Gantry* attacks commercial exploitation of people by evangelical religions. Based on the book by Sinclair Lewis written in 1927, the film was made in 1960; despite being 30 years apart, and the film now 40 years old, the theme still has resonance. When Terence Davies filmed *The Neon Bible* in 1995 from John Kennedy Toole's novel, the revivalist preacher exudes a sinister, exploitative presence. Yet Hollywood has, as often as not, been drawn to the positive qualities of Baptist culture rather than its contradictions. Indeed the unsympathetic portrayals are less effective as critiques than films that strive to take a more inside view. In any case, the Baptist faith still retains its power in American culture. One idea in *O Brother, Where Art Thou?* is that the South has changed, for at the climax of the film the flooding of a backwoods valley by the New Deal programme of the 1930s in order to bring hydroelectric power conveys the idea of illumination coming to the South, both actual in terms of electric light but also spiritual, illumination leading to an enlightenment. Yet at the same time it has not changed, for its Baptist roots go very deep. An enthusiasm for the Baptist message persists and *The Apostle* shows how alive the Baptist spirit remains.

The making of *O Brother, Where Art Thou?* by Joel and Ethan Coen takes as its starting-point Preston Sturges' *Sullivan's Travels*, a comedy about Hollywood mores, which gains considerable depth by switching during its course from the facetious to the serious and then back again. It concerns a Hollywood director of light comedies, John L. Sullivan, who wants to make a message film about the plight of the poor called 'O Brother, Where Art Thou?' and decides to research his subject by masquerading as a hobo. This experiment proceeds as planned to the point where he feels he has done enough and in a final gesture he goes to a group of tramps to hand out five-dollar notes as a form of thanks. Flashing his riches, he is robbed, subsequently arrested and put into jail where he ends up in a work gang. From posing as downtrodden, he learns what it means to be the real thing and to face the sadism and cruelty of the penitentiary. In a moment of compassion, the prison warden allows the prisoners to attend a black church where the preacher has devised an entertainment for his congregation, to be shared with those 'less fortunate than ourselves', instructing them not 'to make our guests feel unwelcome . . . for we's all equal in the sight of God.' To the spiritual 'Go Down Moses' the convict gang shuffle in to take their seats at the front. A Disney cartoon is shown which unites convicts and congregation in laughter, and finally Sullivan too. The comic, like religion, can bind the races and dull the pain of poverty. When Sullivan secures his release, he drops his plan for a socially aware film and goes back to making frivolous comedies.

In picking on the title of Sullivan's fatuous project for their own film, the Coen brothers pay homage to Sturges' abilities as a writer to peer behind the identities people create for themselves. In addition, *O Brother* is a very knowing film about films in general. The Coens bring Sturges' film directly to mind but also several others: John Ford's *The Sun Shines Bright* in which the politicking of Judge Priest in Kentucky, which Ford portrays affectionately, is echoed in the cynical and empty election campaigns of Pappy O'Daniel and Homer Stokes. The appearance in *O Brother* of small-town bank robber Baby Face Nelson mirrors both the reality of Depression-era America but also Hollywood myth-making. *Bonnie and Clyde* is the most famous example but it is a precursor that the Coens have in mind: Don Siegel's *Baby Face Nelson* in which Nelson's irrationality finds an outlet in violence. This is given a comic twist in *O Brother*, where Baby Face is a mixture of absurd extremes: of manic depression at the thought of being known as Baby Face rather than George Nelson, of a murderous *joie de vivre* when he has a machine gun in his hand, and of comic hysteria – 'Jesus saves, but George withdraws' – as he roars at the cowed victims of a bank robbery. At the prospect of being hanged by a mob he exults: 'I'm George Nelson, and I'm feeling ten feet tall.'

The Coens may also have had in mind Elia Kazan's *Wild River* about a cussed old woman refusing to give her home to the Tennessee Valley Authority which wants to flood it in a project to build a hydroelectric dam, a story of opposition between old South and new South that the Coens make into a key theme. Finally, the chain gang – that penal institution so rooted in its home but to outsiders so strange and repellent – turns up in both *Sullivan's Travels* (where Sullivan finds himself in a gang) and *O Brother*. Both Sturges and the Coens probably have in mind a celebrated 'message movie' of the 1930s, *I Am a Fugitive from a Chain Gang*, whose narrative trajectory is the opposite of Sullivan's in *Sullivan's Travels*: a man wrongly convicted of murder suffers life in a chain gang until he escapes and makes a successful career, only to land back in prison when his identity is uncovered. Its message is that the institution is a barbaric one that demeans humans and society ought therefore to abolish it. By contrast Sturges and the Coen brothers take it as a Southern fact of life, reflecting its culture of damnation.

Damnation implies salvation and it is this idea that the Coens put at the heart of their story. It may be a black comedy about prison, about charlatans, about corrupt politicians, about the Ku Klux Klan, even about racism. It may be a musical, featuring revivalist singing, the blues, bluegrass and rustic fiddling. Yet before both of these it is about the polarity between prison, literal and metaphorical, and freedom, literal and metaphorical. Its story is of a trio of convicts, Ulysses Everett McGill, Delmar O'Donnell and Pete, who, having just escaped from the chain gang, hear a prophecy that they will travel a long road but find in the end a fortune, 'although not the one they seek'. They then set off to find the loot, which Everett tells them he has hidden from the robbery that landed him in jail. On the way they meet Pete's cousin, Washington Hogwallop, who removes their chains then betrays them 'for the bounty', Tommy Johnson who has 'sold his soul' to the devil at the crossroads in order to receive the gift of playing the blues guitar, Baby Face Nelson aiming to rob three banks in one day, Dan Teague, the Bible salesman ('selling the truth') who violently robs them. They stumble on Klansmen gathering to hang Tommy and, after helping him to escape, end up on stage at a political rally singing 'I am a man of constant sorrow' to instant acclaim. Pardoned by Governor O'Daniel, Everett, Pete and Delmar are then confronted by the Devil Death who has been stalking them through the film. In an earlier version of the themes explored in *O Brother*, *Raising Arizona*, the Coens had cast a Terminator-type as the Avenger, all bike, leathers, hair and grenades. In the later film, this figure is the more chilling Sheriff Cooley seeking to punish the convicts for escaping, a sinister stereotype of tall, unsmiling, rifle-toting lawman with dark glasses, leather boots and bloodhounds at his heel; above all he is a white man, as Tommy Johnson says, 'with empty eyes and a big hollow voice'. When Everett protests that the Governor has pardoned them, the sheriff replies, 'The Law is a human institution' as if the world of damnation he inhabits has no place for such a puny notion as pardon from a human being, and prepares to hang them. Rescue comes in a wall of water that floods through the woods they are standing in, washing everything away. The prisoners escape to a new life; in particular Ulysses Everett McGill re-establishes his 'bona fides' with the Penelope he married before going to prison and ahead of her chief suitor, Vernon T. Waldrip.

The reference in the names to Homer's *Odyssey* is no accident. When the story is described in the credits as 'based on Homer's *Odyssey*' you struggle at first to connect the epic with 1930s America. But the Coens are both tongue in cheek, relishing the juxtaposition, and serious. Ulysses Everett McGill is a proper Odysseus, travelling a long road to get home again, a quick-thinking charlatan (Homer's adjective for his hero is *polymeetis*, 'of many wiles') who landed in prison not, it turns out, for robbery but for the fraudulent practice of the law. As in Homer, Ulysses Everett is central but the Coens enlarge his character by complementing it with the dimwits, Pete and Delmar. Everett's education and enlightenment are tools for survival but it is Delmar who is quicker to salvation. The three are in a wood, eating cooked rabbit and bickering when, in one of those swift changes of mood which characterise the whole

film, singing is heard to come from a procession of white-robed
men and women making their way to the river:

> As I went down to the river to pray
> Studying about that good old way
> And who shall wear the starry crown
> Good Lord, show me the way.
> Sinners, let's go down . . .

Everett voices his scepticism ('everyone's looking for answers')
but Delmar joins in and returns from the river, sluiced out and
shouting: 'the preacher's done washed away all my sins . . . and
heaven everlasting's my reward'. There is a Homeric reference
here to the land of the lotus-eaters in the *Odyssey*, where some of
Odysseus' crew taste the lotus and lose all wish to return home
– similarly baptism annihilates the past. As Everett remarks,
Delmar is a 'lily of the field', a 'paradigm of hope'. In contrast
Pete suffers from a 'general attitude of negativity'. It is Pete who
thinks he is capable of leading the group (as he says to Everett:
'who elected you leader of this outfit?') but never puts it to the
test and who succumbs to the sirens' song. It is Pete who Delmar
thinks has been turned into a toad for fornicating with the
sirens; even Everett resorts to arguing that this is a judgement on
his character.

Everett's rationalism is undercut throughout the film. When
he says that everyone is looking for answers, he has none of his
own except to pursue the chimera of reunion with Penelope.
When their travels end in cleansing waters that wash away all
troubles, the Coens throw in another Baptist metaphor. This
scene near the end links back to one near the opening when the
blind seer on the handcar (Tiresias) prophesies not only that
they will find a fortune after travelling a long and perilous road
but also that among other 'startlements', 'you shall see a cow on
the roof of a cotton house'. Floating in the lake Everett concludes his speech about the virtues of electricity over miracles
but is taken aback by the miraculous fulfilment of Tiresias'
prophecy: a shack drifts by with a cow standing on its roof.

This is a comedy with a happy ending, sending the audience away uplifted by laughter (as Sullivan had discovered) but the threat of damnation is constant, even when made comic. The grimness of prison, of life on the road and of economic poverty is sketched in rather than paraded before our eyes. The most sinister presences are the avenging Sheriff Cooley, the Ku Klux Klan and Homer Stokes' fear of miscegenation. But the Coens are anxious also to convey wonder. The absurdity of character and of circumstance is offset by the golden colour-wash with which their cameraman, Roger Deakins, has depicted the Mississippi landscape. Also, the film contains several versions of Utopia: Everett's happy family (with Penelope and four daughters), Pete's dream of being a *maître d'* in a hotel, Delmar's of buying a family farm. In the song over the credits, 'Big Rock Candy Mountain', a hobo expresses his dream of the good life: 'You never change your socks, and the little streams of alcohol come trickling down the rocks . . . The jails are made of tin, and you can walk right out of 'em as soon as you are in . . . Where they've hung the jerk who invented work, in the Big Rock Candy Mountains.' Tommy Johnson buys paradise from the Devil so he can play the guitar. Sheriff Cooley calls the noose a 'stairway to heaven'. When the flood overwhelms them at the end, the accoutrements of Everett's home (hair pomade, tyre-swing, gramophone horn) are whirled through the water in slow motion as if in a satisfying dream. Finally the Baptist vision of paradise is the purest: 'I'm going to wear that robe and crown, show me the way.'

Music is the natural outlet among poor communities for creative expression, a means of briefly abolishing suffering. For the different peoples who came to inherit the southern states of America, nowhere was this relief more necessary, and the gift of creating it more abundant, than among the black communities. If there is a missing musical dimension in *O Brother* it is in this respect. It shows the field hollering which the blacks brought to the chain gang and in the blues played by guitarist Tommy Johnson (Skip James' 'Hard Time Killing Floor Blues') the Coens pay tribute to that particularly plangent expression of alienation. The music they omit is the gospel singing and the spirituals of the black church, the context in which Sturges sets his version of salvation in *Sullivan's Travels*. It is one of the fascinating strands of American religion that at first the white European missionaries of the eighteenth century found North America to be a fruitful harvest field. Then, the growth of the black churches, one institution in American life over which black people could exercise control, led to a heartfelt and uninhibited expression – beyond the white man's imagination – of the merits of conversion. Finally, when in the twentieth century Americans began to explore the richness of this tradition, black forms of expression began to feed themselves into white religion. For a faith that laid stress on the visible evidence of conversion, this was a godsend. There could be no more outward means of expressing personal salvation than to engage in the revivalist shouting which the blacks had mastered.

Robert Duvall's film *The Apostle* mines this idea to the full. Right at the beginning it shows Sonny Dewey as a young boy listening to a black revivalist preacher. The child is father of the man: Sonny devotes his life to ministry in the proper style, which accepts no authority but that of God as it is expressed in scripture. Made at the end of the twentieth century, *The Apostle* is a valuable depiction of contemporary religion in a corner of America. Yet it is also a critique of that religion: Sonny's religious convictions come from a character in which inner human complexity and outward certainty struggle in tension with each other. He seems to be in total control but the narrative hinges on a moment when he loses self-control.

Sonny is a well-established, full-time Baptist minister in suburban Texas, married and father of two children, who discovers his wife Jessie is having an affair with a youth minister, Horace. When she wants to separate she manoeuvres the church vote to throw Sonny out of the temple he has established. Tracking his children down to the summer camp that Horace is running and getting into an argument with him, he lashes out at Horace with a baseball bat. To escape a charge of assault, he flees the area,

drowns his car, rebaptises himself as The Apostle and ends up in
Bayou Boutte in Louisiana. There with the help of a local radio
station and a black minister, Brother Charles Blackwell, he starts
a new church and gains a new lease of life. However in the inter-
im Horace has died from Sonny's assault and the law catches up
with him. At the very end he is arrested for first-degree murder
and taken away. Yet the film has not quite ended. As the credits
come up, we see Sonny in a work-party from the penitentiary,
without chains, not breaking rocks, but as they hack away at the
growth by the roadside, still hollering, this time under Sonny's
direction, the refrain of the endless chant is 'Jesus'.

Sonny strides through the film like a colossal monster. The
whole focus is on him so that while the rest of the cast is well
drawn, they are slightly pale by comparison. Jessie is frightened of
him; Horace is just a 'puny-arsed Youth Minister'; Brother
Blackwell's ministry has been defeated by two heart attacks;
Sonny's loyal friend Joe is in awe of him; Toosie, the woman whom
Sonny courts in Bayou Boutte, is coy and uncommitted. The only
comparable figures are the black preachers from whom Sonny has
learnt how to shout. When Blackwell offers him his old church,
now a shack in a field, Sonny comments 'I could do some shouting in here'. His approach to radio preaching is to tell people that
the eleventh commandment 'Thou shalt not shout' does not exist.

The aggression in his religion is enlarged in other ways. Sonny
is shameless: in the opening sequence, he comes across the scene
of an accident on the highway involving several cars and his
immediate response is to find a young man sitting seriously
injured in his car and persuade him in his extremity 'to accept
Christ as his personal saviour'. He is callous in the treatment of
his mother. To Jessie he confesses to womanising, which he calls
his 'wicked wandering ways'. He is a wife-beater judging by the
way Jessie flinches from him as she stands firm in her desire to
split up. The essence of his solipsism derives from his Bible-
bashing. He is always talking, never listening. Even his authority
is self-given; when he rebaptises himself as The Apostle he does
so by himself in the river, as if no one else were fitted to the task.

Yet Duvall's story is much more than that of a misbehaving minister. The second half of the film, after The Apostle has arrived at Bayou Boutte to start a new church, is a vivid portrait of a small community among whom he exercises a genuine charisma. The relationship with the black minister, Brother Blackwell, is warmly drawn; the energy with which The Apostle works to involve white and black, young and old, to repair and repaint the church and its bus is genuine. His capacity for violence is given a righteous outlet when he fights a man who accuses him of consorting with 'a bunch of niggers'. He is courteous in his courting of Toosie, the receptionist at the radio station. He even admits to a feeling of repentance when he prays that Horace might live. This second half is a balance of the first, our revulsion at his monstrousness tussles with awe at his Bible-induced energy to create a community.

To those of no religion or of a different version of religion, the preaching of *The Apostle* seems utterly exotic. This film, financed by Duvall, written and directed by him, and featuring him in the central role, has been a lifetime project. Duvall has been a noted Hollywood actor with extensive credits first in television then in film since about 1960. He is by profession an actor and one of the ways in which *The Apostle* works is as a documentary on acting. Duvall adopts a simple style of filming. The camera records the scene; it is a tool of narrative, not a protagonist in its own right. The people on the screen include not just the professionals playing the major roles but also the host of minor characters including actual preachers, faith healers and pentecostalists. Near the beginning Duvall shows Sonny as a member of a Tag Team in a rousing performance at a tent meeting. Duvall as Sonny is the professional actor but the others are all real-life ministers. The team comprises five whites, two blacks – two females, five males. Professional and amateur merge: they are all performers of a particularly ostentatious kind.

We end up with a vivid slice of Americana. The story becomes a pretext and the film's aim is to record this outsize version of living by faith. It is rooted in history too. When the pioneers moved west in the nineteenth century, Baptist ministers driving into new mission fields were in the van. Over 100 years on, Sonny Dewey, the self-styled Apostle, is no different: he is a nomad in settled America, to whom his fellow-citizens are still to be endlessly converted, endlessly to renew acceptance of Jesus Christ as their personal saviour.

If Sonny is the charismatic but suspect minister, no such nuances surround the character of Harry Powell in *The Night of the Hunter*. He is an uncomplicated embodiment of evil, who lives by murdering widows for their money while masquerading as an itinerant preacher, a serial killer steeped in hypocrisy. The film is justly famous for this characterisation, brought to life by Robert Mitchum, and for its unexpected lyricism, but it is also notable for its picture of the Manichaean struggle between Powell and Mrs Rachel Cooper, evil and goodness in human flesh. Sonny in *The Apostle* is a human being shading his qualities as a leader with a destructive side, while *The Night of the Hunter* is an allegory on these two opposing forces living in two separate people. Like *O Brother* and *The Apostle*, although it is set further north in the United States on the Ohio river, it is an analysis of a state of mind – rural, communitarian, unsophisticated – to which there is no greater authority than the word of God.

Like *O Brother* it is a musical in an integrated way: the songs enlarge the narrative without interrupting it. One song in particular is used to mark stages in the action:

Leaning, leaning, safe and secure from all alarms,
Leaning, leaning, on the everlasting arms.

It is Harry's song, his leitmotif, and when at the climax he confronts frail Rachel Cooper in order to get his hands on the money stuffed in the doll, the fact that he has met his match is signalled by the response to his singing: she changes the refrain to its proper version, 'Leaning on Jesus, leaning on Jesus.' The story is set in the time of the Depression. Young John and Pearl Harper witness the arrest of their father Ben for robbing a bank and murdering two people but not before Ben has entrusted the stolen money to John, making him swear not to reveal its whereabouts: it can be his when he grows up. In jail prior to his execution, Ben Harper shares a cell with Harry Powell, in prison for stealing a car, who extracts from him that the money is still at the Harper house. While Harper is executed, Powell is released and resumes his journey as a 'wolf in sheep's clothing'. He sees his next victim as Ben's widow, Willa Harper. Coming to the house, he ingratiates himself into Willa's favours and they marry despite the hostility of young John. This hostility translates into an obstinacy that resists all Powell's attempts to discover from the children where the money is hidden. Harry then murders Willa and is on the point of finding the money when the children escape, make their way to the river and drift by boat downstream. Pursued by Harry they end up coming ashore at Mrs Cooper's house, who adds them to her family of three homeless children. When Harry tracks the household down, she sees his masquerade instantly and confronts him with a gun. When he is shot in the leg, he takes refuge in a barn. There the police arrest him and in his turn, he is sentenced to death. The film ends with Christmas at the Cooper household and the giving of presents.

Its genius as a film is that the story is an armature for an array of stylistic devices, for an imaginative parade of symbols, and for an unleashing of the visual imagination. The director was the English actor, Charles Laughton, in charge of his first and only film, but it was an unusually collaborative effort: Davis Grubb's original novel had been a bestseller, the cinematic potential of which was discerned by the producer Paul Gregory; the writer James Agee was drafted to write a screenplay and the cameraman Stanley Cortez brought a particularly creative eye to the cinematography. The casting was imaginatively done too, not just Robert Mitchum's Harry Powell with LOVE tattooed on the knuckles of his right hand and HATE on his left but also Lillian Gish's Rachel Cooper, who carries out the commandment, 'suffer the little children to come unto me' to the letter. Gish, born in Ohio, was a major star for the director D. W. Griffith in the 1910s. *The Night of the Hunter* is therefore a return to her roots and also, because of the pastoral quality of some of the scenes, a return to her days as a star of the silent screen. Gish/Cooper and Mitchum/Powell are Love and Hate battling for mastery ('the story of right-hand/left-hand'). Both are not what they seem: under Harry's charms seethe disgust and hatred. Under Rachel's frailty and meekness is a determined will, backed up by a readiness to use a gun in the face of evil.

A prosaic recital of the melodramatic narrative does no justice to the menace with which Powell is invested, a quality which the cinema is well suited to convey: it is not just that the chiaroscuro of the black and white film accentuates shadows and makes darkness visible but Mitchum gives a particularly un-settling timbre to Powell's voice and the editing of the story ensures that the children on the run are never far from their pursuing demon. Innocence threatened is a key theme and its gravity has to be conveyed by the constant juxtaposition of the children with Powell, who carries the menace within himself: the man of God turns out to be possessed by the Devil.

Like Duvall's Apostle, Powell is a self-invented minister. Like Sonny, he is manipulative, an ostensible womaniser and homi-cidal. Because his invocation of the Bible is so synthetic, his hypocrisy seems all the more profound. Like Sonny, he is a nomad in rural America until his reputation catches up with him at the end. However, unlike *The Apostle*, with its consistent docu-mentary tone, the style of *The Night of the Hunter* is composed in different layers: the daytime scenes have an everyday outdoor quality, while the night-time ones are done expressionistically: instead of filming 'en plein air', Laughton shoots these scenes in the studio, simplifying shapes and manipulating lights and the shadows they throw. But there is a lyrical element as well: in a celebrated sequence, the children drift by boat down the Ohio river. While Pearl sings, we see the creatures of the night: a spider in a cobweb and a frog. During the day, while the children stop at houses and call for food, Harry is close behind, keeping up appearances by sermonising among the peach-pickers. Then the film reverts to the night scene and expands it: an owl appears, a tortoise, hares. Sheep watch the boat as it drifts. The children go ashore and sleep in a barn. A lullaby is heard: 'Hush little one hush'. We see the cows in the barn, we hear a whippoorwill, and the moon floats in the sky. Then the lullaby is replaced by Powell singing 'Leaning' in the distance. John and Pearl take to their boat again. A cloud obscures the moon; the boat comes into rough water. A fox watches them intently. Then calm water comes again and the children sleep. When the boat drifts ashore, the camera tilts upwards to the stars, signalling the children's arrival at safety. It is a new day, signalled by the cockcrow, when Rachel Cooper finds them and takes them into her shelter. In her own words she is a 'strong tree with branches for many birds'.

It is important to the film's effectiveness as a story that a saviour of some kind counterbalances Powell's ravening wolf. Since the portrayal of goodness in art is less convincing than that of evil, Mrs Cooper may strike us as unreal: she takes in children wandering and homeless in the Depression; she has a gospel-based idea of the innocence of children, expressed in the sincere but sickly phrase 'children are man at his strongest – they abide'; she instantly sees through Powell's persona as preacher; she carries a shotgun and uses it on him. Yet for the film to work Powell's devil of damnation needs to be balanced by a fully drawn angel of salvation. The happy ending is therefore made into the happiest imaginable: it is Christmastide, Rachel gives the children presents and snow cocoons the house so that its love is insulated inside. It is a divine version of The End as opposed to the grim human conclusion to the plot that it supersedes: Harry faces justice in the courtroom and the prospect of the death penalty. The guard who will perform the execution comments, 'It'll be a pleasure to hang him.' Walt and Icey Spoon, who had previously succumbed to Harry's charms, lead the lynch mob baying for Harry's blood. We are in the country where even in the twenty-first century 38 states permit capital punishment and close on 100 executions take place every year, the most extreme usurpation of divine judgement that man has invented. Damnation is doled out by humans.

5

Violence

I runne to death and death meets me as fast.
John Donne, Holy Sonnet ('Thou hast made me . . .')

If damnation comes from the judgement of humans, we can only look to God for salvation. It is a key strand in Christian thought that there is a profound version of justice beyond the ability of humans to order themselves and if that is the case, we must therefore rely on a divine mercy if we are to escape the risk of damnation. Hence the human soul awaiting the advent of grace (chapter 6 – Guilty as Sin), hence Joan of Arc's cleaving to faith in God (chapter 9 – Crucifixion), hence our individual experience of resurrection (chapter 10 – Resurrections). Hence the importance of the gospel story (chapter 12 – The Image of Christ) in offering two ways out: resurrection in order to overcome Jesus' cruel and unjust execution and, through the sacrifice of his innocence, redemption from the pain of human sin.

The notion of sacrifice is a long way from clear cut American justice in the movies. In Westerns, the hero makes law with the gun, settling matters not through any judicial procedure but by natural intuition of how corruption is to be dealt with, a gift that both sanctifies his violence and as it were lends him the necessary skill with a gun. Moral superiority translates into a practical one. But Hollywood has created another version of this myth, that of the gangster who uses violence to assert his difference from and antagonism toward ordered society. He is the dark *doppelgänger* of the Western hero and the central protagonist of dozens of films.

In the portentous words of the hard-boiled American director, Samuel Fuller, pronounced in Jean-Luc Godard's *Pierrot le fou*, 'film is like a battleground: love, hate, action, violence, death . . . In one word, emotion.' This is a wonderfully concise description of the gangster film, one of America's notable contributions to popular culture, so popular that many other countries have now taken up the genre. Yet, while being a battleground, it offers a context to explore the suffering of the world not just by the willed evil in living and dying by the sword but also in ideas of guilt, redemption from evil, and ultimate salvation. Although we shall look at examples where these themes are touched on, it is a feature of the genre that they have been largely ignored, perhaps as a result of necessity since the mechanisms of revenge and the conclusion of justice have to be kept at the forefront, as if directors and scriptwriters by and large feel that any consideration of whether these people have any human dignity is an irrelevant one. Questions of right and wrong have been sidelined into formulas of 'good guys' (the cops, at least some of the time) and 'bad guys' (the gangsters most of the time) and because the films' purpose is to seduce the viewer into an involvement with the story regardless of rights and wrongs, their creators are most focussed on entertaining adults in an adult world. One side-effect has been that they have not had any hesitation about putting the gangster film at the forefront of portraying violence on screen, to the point where there seem, 100 years on from the invention of the cinema, to be no taboos left as to what is permitted and the images of violence seem drained of moral meaning.

The starting-point was *Underworld* (1927) and during the 1930s crime films were a staple of Hollywood, especially of the Warner Brothers studio. As a genre, it was eclipsed in the 1940s by the growth of the private eye film. Possibly because of the patriotic dictates of the war, the studios kept stories of organised crime off the screen and focussed their entertainment on the *film noir*, a triangular construct of the lone individual (male), the *femme fatale* and corrupt society. The anti-social ruthlessness and cruelty of the gangster were transformed in the private eye into qualities of self-reliance and the rational use of violence in self-defence and to achieve justice.

In the 1950s and 1960s, the activities of organised crime and the presence of police corruption began to reassert themselves in Hollywood as a matter for social concern. A film like Samuel Fuller's *Underworld U.S.A.* (1961) depicts a society infected by criminal activity from the bottom to the top and it is only cleansed by someone from the inside turning against the organisation, a theme reprised in John Boorman's *Point Blank* (1967). *The Godfather* (1972) and *The Godfather: Part II* (1974) gave new impetus to the public's voyeuristic fascination with the mores of criminals and spawned a sub-genre of Mafia films in which criminal profits are fuelled by drugs as well as the more traditional protection money or crooked property deals, and have in effect been globalised. Some of the time, the forces of law and order exert control and eradicate criminal activity but more often, and more dramatically, it is the gangster who brings judgement upon himself as a result of revenge: his killing is the conclusion of personal violence conducted at the extreme level.

If one persists in asking what moral universe is being portrayed, the answer can be surprisingly complicated. In the 1930s and 1950s, the standard version is that the police root out criminal elements in order that the evil man might get his just rewards. On the other hand, film-makers rely on the mechanisms of dramatic identification to involve the viewer and take the story forward. Study of the criminal is more fascinating to the human psyche. In *White Heat* (1949), the pathologically violent criminal is finally brought low but the total focus is on him as an individual and on analysing his motivation and actions. As spectators, we are bewitched by the sight of badness sucking us into his amorality. The option does exist to tell the story from the policeman's point of view so that the audience takes his side and this is brilliantly exploited by Fritz Lang in *The Big Heat* (1953): when Dave Bannion's wife is killed by the mob he is investigating, his search for justice ceases to be his paid work but becomes burningly personal so that his desire for revenge is the audience's as well.

'Film is a battleground.' The American cinema has been a cinema of action and entertainment, less of ideas. The cowboy, the private eye and the criminal, private professions made public and mythicised by Hollywood, naturally embody the American values of self-reliance. But American film-makers have not been drawn to enlarge this code of self-reliance into a philosophy, to explain individual meaning in a hostile universe, to make a heroic idea. It was left to a Frenchman, Jean-Pierre Melville, to inject an existentialist strain into the gangster film. Melville's Americanophilia extended to ten-gallon hats and gas-guzzling cars as well as a profound respect for American popular cinema, a taste shared with the critics of *Cahiers du cinéma*, the influential post-war film magazine started in 1950. Melville was an independent-minded director, not just in his choice of stories but in his working methods: to find the creative freedom he wanted, he took the risk of producing his films himself, rather than rely on the comforts of spending other producers' money. From 1948 until his death in 1973, he made 13 stylish and intelligent feature films but it was only in the 1960s that he found his personal voice in a cycle of films exploring *le milieu*, a shadowy underbelly to comfortable French society in which the police play cat-and-mouse with professional criminals. In this dark world, it is not the police but mischance and betrayal that bring them low. Of the five films – *Le Doulos, Le Deuxième souffle, Le Samouraï, Le Cercle rouge, Un flic* – it is *Le Samouraï* which exalts the individualism of the criminal to heroic even mythical status. Melville is sharply conscious of the isolation of his protagonists. No feature of the gangster is put on a more superhuman plane than his separation from society and from his colleagues. The

opening credits sequence is made up of a single camera movement slowly pulling back from the wall of a room to reveal the
hero lying motionless on the bed smoking a gitane, while his
sole companion is a bird in a cage sustaining its existence with a
feeble but constant chirrup. We read the motto of the film:
'There is no more profound solitude than that of the samurai,
unless it be that of a tiger in the jungle . . . perhaps.' The jungle
is metaphorical: the lone 'tiger' hunts in the asphalt jungle of
the city and his capacity for survival has evolved from mastering
a hostile environment.

The samurai of the title is a professional hit man, Jef Costello,
who has been commissioned to shoot Martey, the owner of a
nightclub. The narrative begins with Jef stealing a car before
going to murder Martey in his office. The police, following up
the death, round him up and include him in a parade at which
he escapes identification. However, when he goes to meet his
contact for the hit in order to be paid he is double-crossed and
shot in the arm. The pressure is now on Jef, because the police
are continuing to pursue him while Olivier Rey, who commissioned the murder in the first place, wants him bumped off
before they catch him. When he is again cornered by the hit
man trying to kill him, he turns the tables and extracts the name
of his enemy. In a long sequence set in the Paris underground,
he evades a police tail, steals another car, tracks down Rey
and kills him. At the end, going to Martey's nightclub, he is
discovered and killed.

Melville's values are those of a heroic society without gods:
professionalism is important, among the police as well as among
the criminals, but honour between thieves is important as well.
If we look for a villain in Le Samouraï it is Olivier Rey, who fails
to deliver to Jef his side of the bargain, namely payment for the
murder of Martey. The gangsters live in a culture where good and
bad are determined not by guilty conscience but a feeling of
shame that one person has betrayed another. It is a universe in
which any divine providence is absent. Rather it reflects the
agenda outlined by the writer and philosopher Albert Camus

that struck such a chord in French post-war life, a loss of belief
in human purpose and an acceptance of amorality in which
violence and even self-violence are constants. The opening sentence of Camus' *The Myth of Sisyphus* might have been written
for Melville: 'There is but one truly serious philosophical
problem and that is suicide.' The imperative posed by the question 'Why live?' is in the absence of a rational answer met with
the cruelty of 'suicide', extended to include the conscious choice
of death at the hands of another. All of Melville's mature gangster films end with the death of the central protagonist, as if
such a death was a timely solution to the problem of existence,
that the end of the film is the end of the gangster's life because
any extension of it put beyond the audience's imagination, is
literally inconceivable. Melville interrupted his sequence of five
gangster films with *L'Armee des ombres/The Army in the Shadows*
(1969, more fully discussed in chapter 7) about the activities of
a group of French *résistants* to the Nazi occupation. He replaces
the cult of the criminal with the cult of the *résistant* as hero and
finds even in the period of occupation, one of the most morally
problematical periods in French history, an almost unalloyed
heroic quality. Its main character, Gerbier, like his gangster *con-
frères* in the other films, dies at the end because given the choice
between running and being machine-gunned, 'he decided this
time not to run . . .'.

Where is human vulnerability in all this? In *Le Samouraï*
Melville concentrates on the surface: Costello is a narcissist, his
character is as deep as the gesture of checking the brim of his hat
in the mirror. He has a girlfriend whom he uses to provide an
alibi but any spark between the two is suppressed: when the
police harass her for information, her discomfort is emptied of
any emotional content. The rigour of the way in which Melville
denies feeling is yet another logical step he takes with the
American gangster film. The emptiness of his heroes' existence
parallels the emptying of the images of moral purpose.

This makes the Boulting brothers' film of Graham Greene's
Brighton Rock (published 1938, filmed 1947) all the more striking

by contrast. The young hoodlum, Pinkie, catapulted by the death of Kite into leadership of a band of petty criminals in Brighton, is motivated by bravado and the quest for self-preservation but also by something unusual, namely his Catholic upbringing from which he has a fear of judgement and hell-fire. In the film he is played by a young Richard Attenborough, twenty-three at the time and although baby-faced, not as young as Greene's original Pinkie who in the book is only seventeen. His youthfulness adds poignancy to his fear of the torments of hell, as if it imparted a special vividness to the terrors he envisages.

Greene, film critic of the *Spectator* from 1935 to 1940, was especially drawn to the thriller in his early fiction, his so-called 'entertainments', and it is perhaps not fanciful to see the idea of *Brighton Rock* being sparked off by his seeing the American gangster films of the 1930s (for example *Little Caesar*, *The Public Enemy*, *Scarface*) and stirring the brew by an admixture of religious guilt. The US title of the film was *Young Scarface*.

The story is this: in the opening sequence a journalist, Fred Hale, is on the run in Brighton from Pinkie and his gang because he has talked to their leader, Kite, and published sufficient detail in the newspaper for Kite to be killed by a rival gang. Fred tries to befriend Ida, who is among the entertainers at Brighton pier, to provide some sort of protection from his pursuers. When Ida leaves him temporarily to go to the public lavatory, Pinkie catches him and bumps him off in the Tunnel of Love. Now Fred's reason for being in Brighton was to leave cards marked with the name 'Kolly Kibber' in public places, so that people finding them could claim a reward from the newspaper. When he is killed, the gang use the cards to provide an alibi for them-selves. One of these is left in a tearoom by a gang member and is found by Rose, a young waitress. Pinkie is anxious lest Rose tell the police that it was someone other than Fred Hale who had left the card. In a move to silence her, Pinkie befriends Rose who instantly falls in love with him. Pinkie's reactions are mixed: while their shared Catholicism is a bond and he wants to frighten her into not letting on to the police what she knows, Rose's adulation produces a disgust in him, not just with her but also with himself: she is soft when he wants to embody an unflinching ruthlessness.

In the background is Ida, an avenging Fury who, getting no joy from the police in trying to unravel the mystery of Fred's death, takes it upon herself to do so. She tracks down Rose and tries to drive a wedge between her and Pinkie only to impel her all the more strongly towards him. To solve the matter and in order to allay his anguish at the possibility of her betraying him, Pinkie gets Prewett, the gang's solicitor, to marry the two of them on the grounds that a wife cannot testify against her husband. By this time, Ida's pursuit has gained a momentum of its own and in a final desperate act to escape her, Pinkie tries to make a suicide pact with Rose. They are tracked down on Brighton pier where Pinkie, backed into a corner and without the gun he has given her to shoot herself, falls into the sea, while Rose, unable to bring herself to the act of suicide, survives.

The novel is natural material for a film which no doubt would have been made earlier than it was had not the war intervened. John and Roy Boulting were drawn in their film-making to creating, mainly through satire, a critique of British society and institutions: among them *Private's Progress, Lucky Jim, Brothers in Law, I'm All Right Jack, Carlton-Browne of the F.O.* and not forgetting the Church of England in *Heavens Above!*. Greene's novel, with its excoriating dissection of the tawdriness of 1930s seaside Britain, offered ready-made material not just for a thriller but one that peeled away the veneer on society: like the American gangster film, it becomes a vehicle to shed light on a much wider corruption. The resulting film is notable for the opening sequence of Hale being chased through the streets and seaside attractions, anxiety amidst jollity, and owes something in its methods to Italian neo-realism, newly arrived in Britain after the war, which encouraged film-makers to use the street as a location rather than the studio. It also helped launch Richard Attenborough's career and the shabbiness and weakness of his fellow gang members are well characterised. Notable portraits are of the solicitor Prewett (Harcourt Williams), clapped-out, compromised, alcoholic, and in particular of Ida (Hermione Baddeley), the blowzy showbiz entertainer whose 'big breasts bore their carnality frankly down the Old Steyne', who 'belonged to the great middle law-abiding class' and who 'had no more love for anyone than they had'. In the book she elicits particular venom from Greene's pen. Despite or perhaps because of Baddeley's whole-hearted performance, the film does not properly capture Greene's hatred towards her. However the script, on which Greene himself collaborated with Terence Rattigan, does convey the startling contrast between Ida's pursuit of right on the one hand and on the other Rose and Pinkie, bewitched by good and evil and the possibility of divine mercy even for the corrupted. When Ida says to Rose, 'I know one thing you don't. I know the difference between right and wrong,' Rose realises that she is right, but thinks to herself that 'their taste was extinguished by stronger foods – good and evil'. She knows Pinkie is evil, so 'what did it matter in that case whether he was right or wrong?' While Greene is far from being explicit, he is taking a swipe at Britain's Protestant institutions based on upholding human justice, which are dwarfed in his mind by divine law and the 'appalling strangeness of the mercy of God'.

There is one major and notorious discrepancy between novel and film. Rose and Pinkie pass a kiosk inviting trippers to 'make a record of your own voice'. Rose insists on Pinkie making one for her as a keepsake. He demurs at first but when he agrees goes into the kiosk on his own and records the following message: 'You asked me to make a record of my voice. Well, here it is. What you want me to say is I love you. Here's the truth. I hate you, you little slut. You make me sick. Why don't you get back to Nelson Place and leave me be?' Although Rose takes the record home her slavish illusions remain intact because having no gramophone she is unable to play it. In the novel, after Pinkie's death and the words of comfort Rose receives from the priest, she goes home to play the record. The final sentence reads: 'She walked rapidly in the thin June sunlight towards the worst horror of all.' Yet when it came to determining an end for the film, Greene had to be persuaded to drop the bleakness of this ending. Instead by a creative stroke of great ingenuity, we see Rose playing the record but the needle sticks on 'What you want me to say is I love you – I love you – I love you'. The final image is of a crucifix on the wall (did Bresson have this in mind when he ended *Diary of a Country Priest* in the same way?). So, the same story has two endings, one ambiguous, one shocking, either touching (Pinkie keeps saying to Rose 'I love you') or terrible (because Rose will one day move the needle on and hear the whole message). For cinema audiences, commercial considerations dictate the need for happy endings so that people leave on a note of uplift. Novels could get away with being more sophisticated, if that is the right word to apply to the nastiness of Greene's original conception. Yet there is something dissatisfying about this nastiness and something satisfying about the ambiguity of the film version. Pinkie is damned but despite his viciousness the stuck record endlessly repeating 'I love you' hints at something loving and innocent within him trying to find a means of expressing itself.

The conjunction of a Catholic setting and gangsters brings to mind the Mafia, a small but highly newsworthy element of Italian culture and its Italian-American counterpart. The Italian origin of gangsters in Hollywood was touched on occasionally in such films as *Al Capone* (1959), a biographical picture with Rod Steiger as a Capone whose Italian-ness was characterised by his devotion to Italian opera, but it was with *The Godfather* directed by Francis Ford Coppola from the novel by Mario Puzo that Italian-ness refracted through an American lens took centre stage to the extent of being an integral part of the Mafia's subsequent reputation. The gangs are organised into families, or rather Families, and family rituals conducted through the Catholic Church form an essential counterpoint to the brutality of the surrounding action, making it more vivid rather than less. Two bravura sequences from *The Godfather* and *The Godfather:*

Part II may be singled out. Crosscutting between scenes, i.e. juxtaposing two theatres of action and cutting back and forth from one to the other in sequence was discovered early on in the history of the cinema as an especially effective cinematic device to intrigue the audience and to heighten drama. *The Godfather* concludes with Michael Corleone's 'settling of family business' by crosscutting between the baptism of his son and heir in church and the serial assassination of rival gang-leaders. In *The Godfather: Part II* Vito Corleone, a young Italian in New York at the turn of the century, begins his career towards Don-hood by carrying out the private assassination of the Black Hand who is tyrannising the neighbourhood. He does so during the Feast of the Assumption when the image of the Madonna is carried through the streets, the public and cacophonous ritual balanced against the revelation of Corleone's ruthlessness and silent, secret cunning. However, while Coppola is intrigued by the coexistence in the Mafia of religious family values (after the killing of the Black Hand Corleone rejoins his family on the street as though nothing had happened) and the uninhibited use of violence in order to secure power, the paradoxes and contradictions of this position are not taken further.

The Coppola/Puzo films did give rise to a number of Mafia movies, among which is *The Funeral*, directed by Abel Ferrara and written by Nicholas St John. This lends a much darker tone to the idea of the Mafia family and indeed mounts an assault on the glamour in which the Mafia movie is often dressed. An earlier film by Ferrara, *Bad Lieutenant*, which inhabits the territory of the exploitation film as much as of the crime genre, had been about a policeman depicted as if made from the same mould as the gangster: he has a family, but is a fornicator and a pornographer; he is employed to enforce the law on drugs, but is an addict himself; he is a gambler who learns nothing from his losses and is evasive about paying his debts. Yet when he investigates the rape of a nun by two young hoodlums in front of the church altar, his Catholic conscience is stirred. In a world of depravity the bad lieutenant of the title is roused to confess his badness before a vision of Christ by fantasising about the act of violence to the nun. He tracks down the perpetrators, lectures them on the awfulness of their crime, then because the nun has herself released them by an act of forgiveness, he too lets them go by putting them on a bus and ordering them out of town. He orders justice as he judges best but some divine spark prompts him not to enforce retribution. As it turns out, this act of mercy is no guarantee of earthly salvation, for in the final scene he is assassinated for reneging on a gambling debt.

The Funeral likewise takes up the theme of the 'strangeness' of divine justice. The story concerns the relationship between three brothers, Ray, Cesarino (or Ces) and Johnny who run a gang in the 1930s. The film is given a suburban rather than a big city setting. The funeral of the title is that of Johnny, the youngest brother, shot down in front of the cinema from which he has just emerged. The coffin sits in the front room of Ray's house and the narrative revolves round it punctuated by flashbacks to past incidents in the lives of the three brothers. It transpires that they are sons of an Italian immigrant who brings them up as gangsters before committing suicide. In one scene we are shown Ray, barely a teenager, obeying his father's order to shoot a traitor tied up and on his knees in front of him. He therefore grows up as natural heir to his father's small but brutal empire. Cesarino is ebullient, emotional and subject to fits of violence. Johnny is a communist (an original touch – Ray is obliged to correct someone who calls him an anarchist) and a philanderer. His death causes a proper grief to his brothers, their wives and his girlfriend, and it inevitably triggers a search by Ray for the killer. This brings Ray into conflict with his wife Jean who regards Johnny's death as a matter for the police or even some other non-earthly judgement: 'Bury him. Let him take his fights with him.' Near the opening of the film, when a priest visits the family in mourning, Ray will have nothing to do with him, but it emerges in the course of the film that while his code as a gangster is driving him to seek an eye for an eye, his upbringing as a Catholic is compelling him to ensure that execution of justice is carried out in accordance with his conscience, in other words not at the expense of someone innocent of Johnny's killing. The prime suspect is Casper, a rival gang-leader with whom they have been negotiating to do business but whose wife Johnny is seducing (three times a week). Ray's gang members want Casper executed but he convinces Ray of his innocence and is released. Meanwhile the real killer has been tracked down by other members and held. It turns out that he is a young mechanic whom Johnny has humiliated by raping his girlfriend in front of him and his friends. When Ray hears this story he is inclined to let the mechanic go: Johnny's murder is fitting punishment for the crime he has committed. But the case goes to retrial, so to speak: Ray takes the mechanic off alone and interrogates him further during which by appealing to God ('Tell me the truth now, the way God sees it') he manages to extract that the young man was only beaten up by Johnny in front of his friends and girlfriend, and that the rape part of the story was invented. Ray gets indignant: 'Do you think you deserve to live? You killed a man. Can you live with that?' He then tells him that his wife is pleading that the law be allowed to take its course, adding that if the rape had been true, then he would have let him live. 'But you took a life; jail is a kindness; I have no choice.' The young man counters that Ray does have a choice, namely not to pull the trigger. Ray: 'But what about my sense of justice?' His victim, arguing for a 'turn the other cheek' mercy, says that he has a choice to do something good or something bad 'which is better than justice' but Ray, fixated on an eye-for-an-eye moral code, ends the argument by shooting him.

This is a critical point. Ray's victim pleads that Ray can choose to go beyond justice, beyond his obsession with right and wrong (shades of Ida in *Brighton Rock*) to doing something good, namely sparing his life. Our first idea is that the film's point of view supports Ray in his act of retribution because immediately on the mechanic's execution, the director cuts to a flashback showing how he had killed Johnny in cold blood, with the result that the two deaths are juxtaposed, one apparently compensating for the other.

As it turns out this is not the denouement of the film. While the way is open to a final scene of tranquillity, Johnny's body being laid to rest and the film ending on a sense of closure, what actually happens is shocking and a great deal more exciting. It is a new morning and Ray casually tells Ces as he shaves, 'I found the people who did it.' Ces nods, leaves, goes and has a drink, reflecting on the fraternal closeness of the brothers through a flashback to all three in high spirits at a party, then goes to bury the mechanic's body. When this is done, the camera tilts up into the sky, cuts and then in a new tilt comes down from the sky to Ray's house. Ces drives up, enters the house, shoots two gang-members in the kitchen in front of the women, goes to the coffin and pumps the corpse of Johnny twice; when Ray appears to investigate the commotion, Ces shoots him in the chest, then sits down and declining the pleas of his wife to give her the gun, shoots himself through the head. In the last shot the wives grieve over the corpses.

This Grand Guignol scene, a staple of Mafia gangster films, has a remarkable resonance. There is a visceral reaction of shock before this violence but dramatically it is of crucial importance. Ces seems to have acted arbitrarily and irrationally but he is in fact a vehicle of divine vengeance. The sense of closure is the ultimate one: this cruel, selfish, violent, self-hating family is finally eliminated from the earth and its power brought to an end. It is a tendency of the gangster film to invest the lives of their protagonists with glamour. They draw an audience both out of a prudish voyeurism to see how the criminal classes live but also to identify with their flamboyance and self-expression. *The Funeral* deliberately destroys the glamour: the brothers when not on business lead dull and respectable suburban lives. While Ferrara gives them one attractive feature, namely their fraternal solidarity, his drift is that they will all from henceforth rot in hell (a judgement on his future which Ray articulates in his clear-eyed way), but as brothers.

Police and gangsters, cops and robbers: frequently in the cinema the two mirror one another, as if the forces of law and order are ultimately as corrupted by human sin and fallibility as the criminals they are bent on pursuing, and that right and wrong are out of kilter with good and evil. This theme of human versus divine law was a major preoccupation of Dostoevsky's. His experience in a Siberian prison, which he analysed in *The House of the Dead*, revealed to him the ordinariness of those people society locks away, often for terrible crimes. For Dostoevsky that 'ordinary' human quality includes the complicated emotions and ideas common to all people. From this he fashioned the first detective story and perhaps the greatest: *Crime and Punishment*. Onto this story of petty murder he plates a story of redemption. Like the two Ferrara films, Dostoevsky's pulp fiction of a murder and its resolution turns into a story about divine justice, albeit in a more epic, more original and more psychologically exact way. It has spawned several cinematic versions, some faithful and some taking a more imaginative route to bringing out its universal quality. We examine two of them in the next chapter.

6

Guilty as Sin

Come let's away to prison, we two alone will sing like birds i' th' cage.
Shakespeare, King Lear, Act 5, Scene 3

Three stories: firstly, a student murders two women and then is gradually overwhelmed with such anguish that he is finally compelled to confess his guilt. When he is sent into penal servitude, the young girl with whom he has fallen in love, follows him there and rescues him. The second story is of a pickpocket, who having learnt and mastered the tricks of the trade, then decides to go straight in order to help a young unmarried woman with a child to bring up. At this point he is caught in a police trap and arrested; sent to prison, he is saved by the young woman who continues to visit him in prison. The third is of a male prostitute who in his cruising encounters the wife of a politician. She falls in love with him and at the same time he finds himself being framed for murder and found guilty. Sent to prison, the woman visits him in prison and sets in motion a legal process to free him.

A common thread to all three stories is a cat and mouse game between the main character and an inspector of police. As they keep crossing each other's paths, the latter tries to trap his victim, who tries disdainfully to fend off his pursuer, bolstering himself with a theory about the right of certain individuals to live beyond the law. Finally all the stories are clearly located by their authors in the big city, respectively St Petersburg, Paris and Los Angeles.

One novel and two films: *Crime and Punishment* (1865–6), *Pickpocket* (1959) and *American Gigolo* (1980). Three authors, Fyodor Dostoevsky, Robert Bresson and Paul Schrader. Three stories with one theme of sin and redemption through love: central to the three is the young woman for whom the hero falls, almost in spite of himself, and who achieves his salvation from crime and sin.

The fountainhead of this religious parable is Dostoevsky (1821–81), the Russian socialist who, following a narrow escape from execution by firing squad, spent eight years in penal servitude in Siberia. It was his experience in prison that awoke in him a religious faith and when he returned to live in European Russia, his nationalism manifested itself in a belief in the need for a religious re-awakening. *Crime and Punishment* is famous for the psychological realism of Raskolnikov's motivations and anxieties after the murder of the old pawnbroker and her sister but it is equally remarkable for its story of redemption: after Raskolnikov is sent to Siberia, the meek Sonia follows him there to wait for his release. His emptiness turns to understanding and love. The rights and wrongs of murder are transcended by an unexpected capacity for human goodness.

Robert Bresson (1907–99), whom we have encountered as the director of *Diary of a Country Priest*, was born in rural France but educated in Paris. His first wish was to become a painter but in the 1930s he began to write film scripts. It was not until the age of 36 that he began making his first feature-length film, *Angels of the Streets*, which gave an early indication of his obsession with human suffering and sin, and with divine salvation. Like a sculptor who cuts and chips away waste material to reveal form, Bresson created a series of perfectly 'carved' films, reducing his stories to a sequence of 'necessary' images, 13 in all between 1943 and 1983. His influences were intellectual rather than cinematic and indeed his style evolved in opposition to the common features of American and European cinema: the star system, big budgets, heavy sentiments. There is a remarkable symmetry to his career. Up to his midpoint film, *Au hasard Balthazar*, he made six feature films about protagonists in claustrophobic settings, including the three that form his prison cycle (*A Man Escaped, Pickpocket, The Trial of Joan of Arc*), one set in a convent (*Angels of the Streets*), and one in the closed world of bourgeois society (*The Ladies of the Bois du Boulogne*). As we have already seen, the rural parish of *Diary of a Country Priest* itself creates an enclosed world. All six films are stories of salvation, which breaks out at the end of each film allowing their heroes and heroines to achieve a release from spiritual imprisonment. When Bresson came to make his seventh feature, *Au hasard Balthazar* in 1966, close to the middle of his forty-year career as a film director, he distilled his intellectual influences to shape a story about the life of a donkey from birth to death, the perfect Bresson protagonist: an archetype for the mute, earthly, suffering creatures in his films, who carry within their persons a spiritual quality. What triggered the story in Bresson's mind was a 'lightning vision' of a film with a donkey as its central character, 'dumb' in the sense of being deprived of speech and supposedly 'dumb' in the sense of stupid, but in fact endowed with intelligence, wonderfully photogenic in the head and importing into the film its 15 minutes of fame as the beast on which the Holy Family fled to Egypt and on which Jesus entered Jerusalem in triumph. The film is pivotal to Bresson's career because it presented in its purest form his ideas of how one person can redeem another – in this case the donkey is a Christ figure bearing patiently the afflictions of the world. It ends with the wounded animal lying down to die surrounded by a flock of sheep: pastoral, peaceable and serene, with the alpine bells on the sheep's necks tinkling a requiem.

After that apotheosis come another six films in which Bresson's austere view of the world threatens to be overwhelmed by pessimism, a world of faith evacuated of hope and love. The act of suicide remains an obsession, taking darker forms still;

redemption becomes more mechanical as though even the senti-
ment inherent in the concept must be jettisoned. When he
made his final masterpiece *Money* in 1983, about the corrosive
effects of money, chief catalyst of human sin, the innocent Yvon,
brought to prison by the transgressions of others is deserted there
by his wife Élise in a wilful inversion of the situation
in *Pickpocket* where Jeanne/Sonia remains faithful to Michel/
Raskolnikov even when he is sent to prison. Towards the end of
the film, Yvon performs a series of axe-murders as though he
were a Raskolnikov gone to the bad, then right at the end, he
performs the confessional act by turning himself into the police,
a procedure which Bresson films in mechanical middle distance
shorn of all hint of emotion. Compare the way Raskolnikov
screws up his courage to go to the police station for 500 pages.

The third *auteur*, Paul Schrader, was born in 1946 in Grand
Rapids, Michigan, USA and brought up in the community of the
Dutch Reformed Church. Forbidden films and TV as a child, he
saw his first film at the age of seventeen. He then embarked on
a turbulent student career in intellectual rebellion against his
father, his upbringing and his country. At Calvin College he took
up journalism, reviewing films and being radicalised by the
movement against the Vietnam War, while he studied Calvin,
Buber, Heidegger and others. In 1968 he went to film school at
the University of California and crystallised his ambitions to be
a film critic. It is striking that his intellectual revolt did not bring
down the guillotine on his religion. He turned his back on the
Church as an institution but his best reviewing focussed on the
way film could be a medium for spiritual ideas, a period which
culminated in 1972 in the publication of *Transcendental Style in
Film: Ozu, Bresson, Dreyer*, an idiosyncratic book from which we
learn as much about the author's preoccupations as about the
three film-makers he examines. Among the ideas he formulates
is one of how the 'transcendental film' moves from 'abundance'
to 'stasis'. This occurs when it achieves the release for the main
character from a set of circumstances: the audience, carefully
channelled and nurtured to this point, experience the moment

as one of transcendence. This religious drive in his critical writings then metamorphosed into a creative one. He had already tried his hand at scriptwriting and in the summer of 1972 wrote the script for *Taxi Driver*, filmed by Martin Scorsese in 1975, which marked publicly Schrader's vision of a sinful world waiting to be redeemed. His Christ figure is the unlikely Travis Bickle, a taxi driver whose contact with all the 'scum' of New York in the backseat of his car drives him to a revenge which turns into an act of redemption: he kills the men exploiting Iris, the teenage prostitute, and shocks her into returning to her family, in effect into salvation from sin.

This idea of two Americas, one upright and acutely conscious of right and wrong, the other permissive enough to allow prostitution and pornography to flourish, indifferent to the very idea of sin, continued to grip Schrader, and led him in his second feature, *Hardcore*, to concoct a story which could illustrate this idea in as stark a manner as possible. It tells of a family in the Dutch Reformed Church in Grand Rapids, whose daughter on a church youth camp in California absconds and finds herself taking part in pornographic films. The father, Jake Van Dorn, is then obliged to leave the security of his community and go to California to look for his daughter, a land whose milk and honey have become the fruits of hedonism. Coming face to face with the intricacies of the sex industry, he enlists the help of Nicky, who is performing at a club called Les Girls (advertising a live 'nude-in'), in order to find his daughter. In one potent scene at the airport, Jake and Nicky discuss religion. Nicky happily admits to membership of the Venusian Church and when Jake expounds a pure Calvinism ('I believe in TULIP' – Total depravity, Unconditional election, Limited atonement, Irresistible grace and the Perseverance of the saints) Nicky shrewdly asks, 'Before you can become saved, God knows who you are?' to which Jake replies that he would not be God if he did not know the names of those who will be saved. Nicky responds with scorn, 'It's all worked out, fixed . . . and I thought I was messed up.' She is not, on this line of reasoning, about to give up the Venusian Church. The film, which contains echoes of the morality of the Western and of the private eye movie in its portrayal of the hero resolving his crisis outside the law, by using his own strength physical and mental, descends into violence, with Schrader disturbing his liberal audience by hinting at the darkest side of pornography: murder can be filmed as a means to sexual gratification. The film needs a bleak ending to match the bleakness of his vision, a reworking of the parable of the prodigal son in which the son resists the father's act of forgiveness. Instead Schrader seeks to create a transcendent moment: at first his daughter resists Jake's decision to take her back home but she succumbs when he says to her 'You take me home.' Yet we sense that no reconciliation has occurred and, furthermore, when he abandons Nicky to the streets, he doubles our repugnance. The moment of stasis is empty.

It is this delicate idea of final reconciliation that Schrader strives to bring to life in his next film *American Gigolo*, which like *Hardcore* is from his own screenplay. *Hardcore* has the virtue of an autobiographical film, an intense telling of Schrader's move from the Dutch Reformed Church to a 'free' life in California, but also the vice, that he fails to find an imaginative way to resolve the story.

What gives *Crime and Punishment* a universality is the vulnerability of the murderer, Raskolnikov. In *Hardcore*, Jake Van Dorn is a loner who resorts to the fist and the gun to make his own law. The main character therefore imposes a resolution to the story, instead of it overwhelming him unexpectedly. For *American Gigolo*, Schrader created a central character who like his forerunners, Raskolnikov in *Crime and Punishment* and (as we shall see) Michel in *Pickpocket*, believes with seeming confidence that he can exercise his will to create the outcome he seeks, but in reality is prey to far larger forces shaping his destiny. When Julian Kay (named after Kafka's Joseph K in *The Trial*) steps from self-absorption and turpitude onto the path of salvation, when he experiences the epiphany of the loveless boy redeemed by love, Schrader achieves a more satisfying ending than in *Hardcore*. The film marks his coming of age as a director.

So, three authors and three stories, three crimes and three criminals. Raskolnikov's crime is specific, premeditated murder, not just of the 'superfluous' pawnbroker but of her innocent sister Lizaveta as well. The act is described in brutal detail. In *Pickpocket* on the other hand, Michel's criminal activity is petty, even though at points it achieves heights of poetry. His pickings are poor at first, but once he joins up with two other professionals, sharpens his technique and perfects his training, the ballet of hands in motion which Bresson choreographs to show the three pickpockets at work in the Gare de Lyon is a justly celebrated sequence, endowing these thieves, or at least their hands, with a grace that seems divine in origin, the beauty of the means justifying the criminal ends – for a brief moment. In *American Gigolo* Schrader echoes this in the shots of love-making, adding an extra dimension to a gratificatory scene. When Julian makes love to Michelle for the second time, the scene is filmed as a series of deliberate and sensuous limb movements. It echoes, not just the pickpocketing in *Pickpocket*, but the cool and clinical sex sequence Jean-Luc Godard filmed in *A Married Woman*. Since Godard was brought up in Geneva, Calvin's city, the two sex scenes could be considered to constitute a Calvinist sex manual.

These are surfaces. The internal state of mind in all three stories is more significant. Raskolnikov's brain mixes up a burning desire to confess his crime, a philosophical defence of why the pawnbroker did not deserve to live, and a compassion for the predicament of Marmeladov's family, he drunk and jobless, his wife Katerina Ivanovna consumptive, and Sonia the daughter driven to prostitution to support the family and its three young children. In *Pickpocket*, Michel's circumstances are less confused: he does not want to work nor look after his dying mother and turns to petty crime, less as a means of survival than because pickpocketing is the only activity to arouse his interest, a sort of drift towards damnation. In *American Gigolo*, Julian's activity is within the law but his prostitution is a triumph of body over soul, matter over spirit, and lovelessness over love. When he is caught up in the enquiry into the murder in vicious circumstances of a client, a crime for which he is framed but for which near the end it is specifically explained he did not commit, the detective (called Detective Sunday in honour of the moral majority) pronounces him 'guilty as sin', in Calvinist judgement on the conduct of Julian's life: he has damned himself already.

So, three criminals and three policemen. The cat-and-mouse game played between them is cast in *American Gigolo* as the conflict of righteousness and sin, in addition to which Schrader hints at another conflict between human and some other kind of law.

> SUNDAY: Doesn't it ever bother you, what you do?
> JULIAN: Giving pleasure to women? Am I supposed to feel guilty about that?
> SUNDAY: But it's not legal.
> JULIAN : Legal is not always right; men make laws; sometimes they're wrong, stupid . . . or jealous.
> SUNDAY : Do you know better?
> JULIAN : Some people are above the law.
> SUNDAY : How do these people know who they are?
> JULIAN : They know. They ask themselves.

Despite a feeling in the spectator that Julian is getting out of his depth philosophically (rather like Nicky at the airport in *Hardcore*), Schrader is honouring the pedigree of Julian's predecessors. When Michel meets the Inspector in *Pickpocket*, he argues for those people, 'intelligent, with talent, even genius', whose 'consciences select them' to break the law. Michel, like Raskolnikov, is both studious and in rebellion against study (books are among his few possessions but they are gathering dust), drawing comfort from the philosophy of the superman: among his books is *The Prince of Pickpockets: A Study of George Barrington* by Richard Lambert (Barrington was an eighteenth-century pickpocket and author, who merits an entry in the Dictionary of National Biography). In this respect, he closely

resembles Raskolnikov, also a student in limbo, to whose philosophy of the right of certain individuals to put themselves above
the law Dostoevsky devotes several pages. These form part of the
discussions with the police Inspector, Porfiry Petrovich, whom
Raskolnikov regards with suspicion for fear of giving himself
away, but to whom he is drawn in order that he might argue in
defence of his theory. On his way to see Porfiry, with his friend
Razumikhin, Raskolnikov thinks to himself: 'Is it a good thing
I'm going there or isn't it? The moth flies to the candle-flame of
its own accord. My heart's thumping, that's the worst of it!'

Particularly in Dostoevsky's version, the Inspector is a secular
confessor. For much of the novel Raskolnikov is on the edge of
blurting out to Porfiry what he has done. In *American Gigolo*, this
element of the story has been lost. It is the mechanics of the
murder inquiry that pitches Julian into the arms of Sunday, not
some inner compulsion. The location of the confessional proves
instead to be prison where in the final image of the film Michelle
Stratton, wishing to touch Julian in compassion, puts her hand
on the glass screen that divides them and Julian leans his head
against it. The positioning of Michelle's fingers and Julian's
bowed head are a blessing of him by her, priestly in its pose and
signifying the moment of Julian's salvation, his resistance to her
love finally overcome.

In this final sequence, Schrader seems to copy *Pickpocket*
closely. Michelle Stratton makes two visits to Julian in prison,
who resists her presence and urges her to forget him, yet when
at the end of the first visit she gets up, he says, 'don't go'; at the
end of the second, he finally confesses: 'My God, Michelle, it's
taken me so long to come to you.' As he speaks an electronic version of the slow movement from Mozart's Clarinet Concerto
begins: as the credits come up we hear an electric guitar taking
up the theme from the organ. As an ending it has the authentic
'transcendental' moment that Schrader identifies in Bresson. Yet
there is a dislocation between the two sensibilities: to finish
Pickpocket, Bresson uses Lully's baroque violins and trumpets to
signal Michel's release from bondage. Schrader no doubt sought

similar musical uplift in Mozart, but either he or his producers insisted on it being scored for electric guitar and rock band. That the uplift therefore has a tawdry quality is perfectly in keeping with Julian's character.

There is another dislocation between the two films. *American Gigolo* uses professional actors with the necessary theatrical skills, notably Richard Gere as Julian; for *Pickpocket* Bresson used non-professionals and for Michel the inward Martin Lassalle, gaunt of visage and clothed throughout in the same shabby suit. Surely prompted by the neo-realist films coming out of Italy after the war featuring ordinary, untrained people from the street, Bresson rigorously excluded trained actors from his films after *Journal* in 1950 and went on to evolve a polemical aesthetic to justify his approach. In a filmed interview in 1965, he defines film acting as not watching or checking oneself, so that words and gestures are spoken and made as if one was an automaton. One glance at a Bresson film shows the effect of the style and because we are so unused to it, it feels at first quite flat, almost repellent. But he uses it in two particular ways. In the interview he quotes, gnomically and unexpectedly, 'Most great battles are fought at the intersections of military maps.' What he is arguing is that the art of *cinematography* (the word is carefully distinguished from the theatrical art of the *cinema*) is in making connections, whether between two pieces of film, between sentences of dialogue, between a person's looks and gestures, even between the beginning and end of a shot, that is, the key element is what happens at the edge where the two elements intersect. Whereas dramatic art 'seals the image so that it can't move' with cinematography the spectator has to use the imagination, to work to create meaning.

Furthermore, this austere style is a means to a particular end. Bresson further justifies this 'flatness' as allowing us to see 'something of the soul, the presence of something superior which is always there, of someone who is God'. This works because of his idea about the grace of God working in people. For us to see it, his 'models' (as he called them, rather than 'actors') need to be obedient to a directing style that strips away the accretions of personality, so that they become vessels awaiting grace. Michel in *Pickpocket* is the paradigm: he drifts through the film in a state of self-absorption until the final shot when he finds the capacity in himself to love another, to signal the presence of grace.

A third difference between the two films is in the subtle way Bresson uses the soundtrack in this final sequence. In *Pickpocket*, Jeanne makes two visits to Michel in prison punctuated by an interval caused by the illness of her child. When she does make a second visit, Michel sees her as transfigured: 'Jeanne, what a strange road I had to take to reach you.' During the interval of her absence Michel asks himself 'why go on living?' in suspense between the heaven of Jeanne's return and the hell of self-damnation. To heighten the moment, Bresson uses the sound of footsteps (as he does in *Journal* – see chapter 2): will they stop outside his door and let him out or will they go past? One of the reasons prison was such a powerful location for Bresson was that in it sound becomes more important than sight: more is learnt by listening than seeing, an aesthetic strategy he was to bring into full play in his films in order to nourish the spectator's imagination (especially in *A Man Escaped*, discussed in chapter 7). When Michel hears footsteps, they are not just the sound of an approaching guard, but of his destiny. His soul is in jeopardy, a word which derives from the French 'jeu parti', a game in which victory and defeat are in balance. When the footsteps finally stop at his door and the key is turned, the audience has its first inkling of the presence of the angel of salvation. Jeanne is not just Michel's confessor but his intercessor as well. Bresson's films are peopled with young girls taking the high road to damnation (an idea he took from Bernanos), but he bestows on Jeanne an innocence, a compassion and a purity of presence that make her a virgin in spirit if not in flesh, like Dostoevsky's Sonia, who while prostituting her body preserves her soul, and by it offers salvation to Raskolnikov.

All three works of art, while concentrating on the travails of a single figure, suggest a larger social corruption. The cause is money. Bresson is clearest about this: the opening image, after a shot of one of Michel's diary entries, is of banknotes being handled at the racecourse, picking up Dostoevsky's idea that Raskolnikov's crime is triggered by the act of pawnbroking, the exchange of goods that impoverishes the customer. Yet it is Schrader who capitalises on the theme most fully. The first conversation in the film is between Julian and his procuress, Anne, and their argument, which undermines their relationship, is about how much Julian is to receive for the job he is given. Julian, in the best commercial manner, defends his right to a decent monetary stake for performing these sexual exchanges. Later on it is the question of money that complicates his first encounters with Michelle.

One final link is the recurrent idea of 'a man and his room'. Raskolnikov spends long hours in his dirty, closet-like flat in St Petersburg, indifferent to his surroundings, like a prisoner 'doing time'. Michel's room is a Parisian version of this cabined existence (a setting which Melville also uses on a slightly grander scale as the home of his samurai gangster – see chapter 5). Schrader had also depicted Travis Bickle's home in *Taxi Driver* on the same lines but for *American Gigolo* he gives the idea a splendid twist. Julian's apartment is beautifully fitted out and his clothes, the tools of his trade, are super-abundant. As the story develops, the searching of their own private rooms, which obsesses Raskolnikov and Michel, in Julian's case is used to mark the turning of his world 'upside down': when the police go through his room, his possessions are tipped and scattered everywhere. It is a crucial stage in stripping Julian of his illusions about the world he inhabits. Pawnbroking, pickpocketing and prostitution point to an unequal relationship between rich and poor, where those who have not try to take advantage of those who have: human sin is a deep reflection of human disorder.

7

Oppression

The prisoner leaps to loose his chains.
Isaac Watts, Hymn ('Jesus shall reign . . .')

There is no crueller product of human disorder than war. The solitary individuals described in the previous chapter struggle against the walls they erect around themselves. For prisoners of war, on the other hand, incarceration is not of their making and they have committed no wrong except that of being on the side of the vanquished. For the existentialists of mid-twentieth-century Europe it was the public oppression of Nazi occupation, felt keenly everywhere, which led to the cogent articulation, especially in France, of a philosophical response. Hence a pessimism incubated during the war grew after it into intellectual doubt about human freedom, and gave enormous currency to a view of the world ungoverned by God, from which the only conclusion could be that he did not exist. Both Robert Bresson and Jean-Pierre Melville were strongly shaped by the experience. Bresson spent time in a prisoner-of-war camp in 1940–41, while Melville was evacuated to England after Dunkirk and served with the Free French forces in North Africa and Italy. When each turned to making a film about France under the occupation, they avoided exact autobiography, but in choosing a narrative, they both made very personal films, to which they could bring some of their own experience and in which their ideas about the meaning of human existence were expressed in the purest form.

Robert Bresson used *Escape from Montluc*, an account by André Devigny of his escape from the German prison at Fort Montluc in Lyons. Devigny had become a *résistant* early on and in 1942 joined the 'Gilbert' network covering the area from Lyons to Toulouse and south-eastern France. In April 1943 he was arrested and imprisoned. Sentenced to death on 20 August 1943, he escaped on 25 August, three days before he was due to be shot. His story was first published as an article in *Le Figaro Littéraire* in 1954 under the title 'Un condamné à mort s'est échappé' ('A man under sentence of death has escaped') and tells of the extraordinary manner in which he did so. This involved dismantling the cell door, making ropes out of blankets and clothes, hooks out of a metal window frame, and calculating an escape route over the roofs and open ground. The enterprise required ingenuity, persistence, luck, imagination and willpower. The suspense is not in the fact of the escape but in the means of escape. Of this unlikely material Bresson makes a religious fable: the drama in our lives is not in the fact of salvation but the means of it.

The clues to interpreting the story in this way are embedded in Devigny's account, for he writes it as a religious story: he tells us that he had become indifferent to religion on growing up, but once in prison this began to worry him. Two relationships became particularly important to him. The first was with the man in the next-door cell, Jeantet, who when first encountered is afflicted with despair and contemplating suicide and whom Devigny rouses from apathy to a point where he is resurrected as a person. The second is with Roland de Pury, a Swiss Protestant minister, to whom Devigny turns for spiritual guidance. It is from de Pury that he receives a copy of Luke 11 ('Ask, and it shall be given you; seek, and you shall find; knock, and it shall be opened unto you.'). In a remarkable passage, he reflects intensely on how the experience of prison brought him face to face with what his life should be: how prayer ceased to be mechanical; how his faith was so sincere 'that the Almighty could not remain insensible to my appeal'; how he had 'made [his] peace with God'; how he was put through such agony 'that I have often wondered whether He was, in fact, on my side'; that he wanted to die 'facing the enemy'; that he never lost heart or surrendered. It is remarkable how Devigny instils Jeantet with a will to live and receives in turn from de Pury the necessary spiritual peace to face up to his ordeal. Even in the harsh confines of Montluc it was possible to forge a chain of community. Devigny is remarkably sensitive to what was happening to him. He boasts of a 'certain congenital predisposition to good luck' but is simultaneously humble enough to discern 'two elements in [his plan of escape]: mine and God's. Where, I wondered, was the dividing line set?' Divine aid would only come 'as I threw every physical and moral reserve I possessed into the balance'.

The publication of this account must have seemed to Bresson like one of those miracles that occur in his films of the 1950s, a chance incident in which the hand of God seems to be discernible. Even the title is compelling, for how better to describe the human condition for a pessimistic Catholic: 'a man condemned (by the Fall) escapes damnation (by means of the grace of God)'. The resulting film, made with Devigny's help, is one of Bresson's purest.

Bresson's religious outlook has been called Jansenist. In his case, Jansenism means that there is an austerity both in the universe and in the way art depicts it, that predestination and chance have an intimate relationship, and that at root he cleaves to the tenet of salvation by grace. So, one's immediate view of Bresson is as a pessimist – life is predetermined – and the natural end is death, including death by one's own hand. Bresson's Catholicism is both maverick, since to endorse suicide is heresy, and orthodox, for while the end is death, it is often serene.

For his part, Jean-Pierre Melville turned to the book by Joseph Kessel, *L'Armée des ombres* (*The Army in the Shadows*) and in doing so interrupted his sequence of five gangster films (see chapter 5), replacing the cult of the criminal with the cult of the *résistant* as hero. Kessel's book, written in 1943, reflected vividly the stories of resistance that were coming out of occupied France. It clothes a narrative under the guise of various episodes from the life of a *résistant*, Philippe Gerbier, working under Luc Jardie. The middle section of the book is called 'Notes de Philippe Gerbier', in effect a journal of entries giving a brief, impressionistic account of acts of resistance. Kessel, aged forty-eight in 1943, a war correspondent by profession and having served in the RAF during the war, was in a good position to collect dramatic stories about what was happening in France. Melville takes this material and shapes it into a continuous narrative beginning in October 1942 and ending in February 1943, a period in which the French population began to turn from support for Pétain and the Vichy government to a vivid detestation of the German occupation.

Bresson's film opens without prevarication: the viewer sees a prisoner (André Devigny, whom Bresson renames Fontaine for the film) in the back seat of a car waiting for the right moment to open the door and run. There are two false starts before a tram finally brings the car to a halt. Seizing the moment, the man jumps out and runs, only to be recaptured immediately by the Germans. The sequence is filmed from inside the car with a restricted field of vision, in which sounds alone without words tell us what happens. It is our imagination that creates the scene.

Compare with this a sequence from Melville's *The Army in the Shadows*. Gerbier sits in the German HQ awaiting interrogation and torture; the German guards are taciturn; the building, a former hotel, is shrouded in silence. Through a whispered conversation with the man sitting next to him he plots an escape. Suddenly action erupts deliberately and precisely. Gerbier kills the guard with a premeditated snatch of the knife from the soldier's boot and the plunging of it into his neck. Both men run. That the anonymous prisoner either dies under a machine gun or escapes we are left to imagine, for we hear only the sound of gunfire, an exact and practical example of Bresson's theory (put into practice in the opening sequence of *A Man Escaped* just described) that the eye is 'in general, superficial, the ear profound and inventive'. Gerbier himself escapes. In order to hide from possible pursuers he plunges breathless into a barber's shop. Will he be betrayed? The barber (played by Serge Reggiani with a wonderfully hangdog wartime look) emerges from his basement, shaves him, and as Gerbier goes, gives him a coat. The escape sequence in the hotel takes four minutes and thirty seconds, and the asylum with the barber some two minutes and forty-five seconds, the two episodes being linked with Gerbier running from the hotel and down a side street, his feet pounding on the pavement, for half a minute. In all that eight minutes less than one hundred words are spoken, the most urgent, when Gerbier urges his fellow prisoner to make a dash for the doors, being conducted in a whisper.

After Fontaine's failed attempt to escape from the car in *A Man Escaped* the rest of the film is devoted to his escape from Montluc prison in an economy of words and precision of gesture similar to the sequence of Gerbier's escape in *L'Armée*. Both are concerned to put the activities of the French Resistance on a heroic plane, but in this common world of oppression and cunning, while Melville recognises a code of honour (Gerbier and the barber: no betrayal), Bresson sees the operation of grace. 'The wind blows where it wills' (John 3:8, REB) is the alternative title for *A Man Escaped*. In Melville the 'wind' is capricious and empty; in Bresson it is spirit bestowing grace. Melville is rooted in the twentieth century, the world of gangsters, brutality and meaninglessness, Bresson both in the twentieth century and outside it. For example, when Melville's Gerbier kills the guard, the spectator is not spared the plunge of the knife in the neck. In *A Man Escaped* Fontaine likewise kills a guard but we are not shown it; we hear only the muffled grunt of the murdered man. Bresson both draws on the dramaturgic tradition of Greek tragedy in which violence reported opens the imagination rather than closes it and also performs an act of delicacy, which is out of sympathy with the contemporary cinema's love of graphic violence, drawing a discreet veil over Fontaine's committing of murder.

Bresson and Melville make a fascinating pair. Bresson was 10 years older and had entered the film industry earlier before making his first full-length film in 1943. Melville, independent in mind and method (like Bresson) made his first film *Le Silence de la Mer* in 1947 quite outside the industry. In doing so, he said that he wanted 'to attempt a language composed entirely of images and sounds, and from which movement and action would be more or less banished. So I conceived the film a little like an opera.' Hence Melville chooses to ensure that his actors behave like statues, so that the spectator concentrates on the face and on the sounds. It is not difficult to see how this would appeal to Bresson searching to banish theatrical manners from the cinema, and for whom gestures, even movements of the eyes, were always deliberate and made significant by the camera frame. Yet when *The Army in the Shadows* appeared in 1966, critics were tempted to call it 'Bressonian', an appellation which sparked comic indignation in Melville in an interview of 1971: 'I'm sorry but it's Bresson who has always been Melvillian.' He argues that Bresson reaches his mature style with *Diary of a Country Priest* and '. . . you will see that it's Melville. *Journal d'un curé de campagne* is *Le Silence de la Mer*', which Melville had made two years earlier.

Yet if there is a stylistic link, and also an attraction to making a film about the facts of the war, the two film-makers interpret them in radically different ways. Melville charts the desperate, comfortless state of humanity, which can only be alleviated by individuals sharing experience and adventure. For Melville God does not exist. Like Camus he believes that chance is 'the only reasonable divinity': good fortune and misfortune are not the results of some guiding hand. By contrast Bresson treats his story as a fable on the operation of the grace of God, drawing on Pascal's *Writings on Grace* (probably written between 1656 and 1658) to exemplify the Augustinian view of free will, as opposed to the Calvinist version (God sent Jesus to redeem those he wished to save and deprive of grace those he wished to damn), or the one he calls Molinist, after Luis de Molina, who had written *The Harmony of Free Will with the Gifts of Grace* in 1588 (God has a conditional will to save everyone, and whether good or bad use is made of this grace is a matter of human will): Devigny has been condemned but escapes the sentence by virtue of exercising his own will aided by that of God.

Both are concerned with heroic France: not the France of collaboration or of response to oppression by sullen indifference or introversion, but with the struggle in seemingly hopeless circumstances of the free human against walls, literal and meta-physical, that deny freedom. In Melville the seven main charac-ters are canonised as types of the Resistance: Gerbier and Mathilde are the loyal commanders in the field; Luc Jardie, 'innocent of arms', directs the grand picture (like the real-life Jean Moulin); Felix and Le Bison are the reliable executors of orders; Jean-François is the good-looking and likeable young man with an instinct for the right cause; Claude Lemasque is uncertain of himself but wants to play his part. Both Kessel and Melville put them on a pedestal. Bresson's story is quite different: although it is Devigny/Fontaine's human imagination that plots his escape, and although he has the moral support of his fellow prisoners, it is divine providence that leads to tri-umph. Compare the two endings: when Devigny/Fontaine and his young companion descend from the outer wall and escape into the cloud of steam enveloping the bridge over the railway, this metaphor for 'assumption into heaven' occurs to the sound of the Kyrie from Mozart's *Mass in C Minor*. In *The Army in the Shadows*, Melville, who (as we saw in chapter 5) was fascinated by the idea of honour and dishonour among thieves with the result that his gangster films hinge on the idea of the 'double cross', makes an ironic and complex version of the double cross the dramatic climax of his war film. The cool and brilliant Mathilde has been arrested and a photograph of her daughter discovered on her person (a photograph which in a previous scene Gerbier had urged her to destroy). The Gestapo immedi-ately know her weak point: Mathilde must tell them the names of other *résistants* or her daughter will be sent to a military brothel in Poland to satisfy German soldiers from the Russian front. When Mathilde divulges three names and is freed in order to allow her to contact other *résistants*, Jardie and Gerbier realise she must be shot before she gives away others. Le Bison revolts at the prospect but is persuaded by Jardie when he tells him that she is in effect asking for death, that unable to commit suicide, she is pleading for execution. In the final sequence a car containing Jardie, Gerbier, Lemasque and Le Bison turns into a street, while Mathilde comes towards it on the pavement. Le Bison shoots her and she collapses in a heap while the camera with the car speeds away from her. Mathilde is 'double crossed' by Jardie and the others, for her own good and that of the Resistance.

Yet even the atheist Melville cannot help investing this episode with an abstract quality, a suggestion of the mystical at the limits of human reason. In the penultimate sequences Gerbier has been sprung from prison thanks to Mathilde's meticulous planning and execution and has spent a month hiding in an obscure house in the country, living in solitary confinement behind closed shutters and not venturing out for fear of being seen. He has swapped one prison for another. Five books have been provided to give mental comfort: not classics, not thrillers, not religious works. Instead, they are written by *le patron* himself, Luc Jardie, his 'saintly' leader. They are works of mathematics and of logic, the fifth being presented to the viewer as the cornerstone: *Transfini et continu* – untranslatable metaphysics, almost mystical works of abstract thought. When Jardie arrives to discuss what to do about Mathilde, he presents it as a mathematical problem, which requires an answer. Le Bison's rebellion against the mathematical solution is based on moral considerations, an inarticulate expression of compassion, which Jardie sets aside by stating that Mathilde is asking for the mathematical solution, which is her own death. Le Bison accepts this but after he has gone Jardie admits to Gerbier that he is in no position to know whether Mathilde is choosing to be executed. Melville reveals a strong sense of honour and of loyalty but none of a divine morality. While Bresson's *A Man Escaped* ends in triumph, *The Army in the Shadows* ends in defeat: a final credit tells us that Gerbier, Jardie, Le Bison and Lemasque were all killed within several months of the shooting of Mathilde.

Interestingly, Bresson might have been drawn to an ambiguous middle ground, for Devigny's original account of his escape from Montluc does not quite end with the escape from the prison. He and his companion are recaptured and yet he escapes a second time, while his companion is never seen again. He sees his recapture as the mockery of God but has the will to break free again and, in doing so, is aided by a stranger: 'God must have sent him, I thought.' One concludes that the pair of film-makers represent two poles of French moral thought, one Catholic, the other divergent and unreconciled, linked by an invisible longitude of a shared past and shared stylistic concerns, two opposite halves of the same sphere.

The Army in the Shadows opens with the recreation of a potent scene from newsreels of the period, that of soldiers of the German Wehrmacht marching down the Champs-Elysées in Paris. We first see an epigraph for the film: 'Mauvais souvenirs, soyez pourtant les bienvenus . . . vous êtes ma jeunesse lointaine' ('Troubled memories, yet welcome all the same: you are my distant youth'). Then, with the camera at ground level, we see a column of German soldiers marching by the Arc de Triomphe and advancing towards the camera, all to the sound of a military brass band playing a melancholy march. Melville recreates this bitter memory of the Germans flaunting their naked military might in the faces of the occupied and does so with style; it both repels and fascinates him. It was shot early in the morning before the traffic started (as indicated by the presence of a floodlight placed high in a tree to assist with illumination). Yet if the newsreel is one precedent for his film, there is another as well, to which Melville makes conscious homage. *Rome, Open City*, made almost 25 years earlier, begins in the dark. There is the sound of German song on the soundtrack; the Spanish steps in Rome's Piazza di Spagna can be dimly seen in the background; a vehicle disgorges a group of German soldiers who proceed to raid an apartment in search of an Italian resistance fighter. The voice of a radio announcer is heard ('London calling Italy') then quickly extinguished as we see Giorgio Manfredi make his escape over the rooftops. When the soldiers search the flat, they find only two old women (crossing themselves and muttering 'Jesu!').

Work on the script for the Italian film had been started in September 1944, three months after Rome's liberation by Allied troops in June, and recalls events under the German occupation of Rome of less than 12 months earlier. Shooting of the film started in January 1945 and it had its premiere in September of that year. Its director was Roberto Rossellini who, like Melville was recalling the troubled times of occupation but unlike Melville doing so while the memory was raw and unmediated by time. After the desperate motivation of Gerbier and Mathilde in Melville's film and the sight of Devigny/Fontaine on a perpetual knife-edge in *A Man Escaped*, it is something of a relief to turn to the full-blooded humanism of *Rome, Open City*, which has two heroes, one the Communist resistance leader, Luigi Ferraris alias Giorgio Manfredi alias Giovanni Episcopo, the other the Catholic priest, Don Pietro Pellegrini. The story is a vivid one with several strands, wonderfully interwoven and brought tragically but satisfyingly together at the end. The main story is the hunt for Manfredi by Major Bergmann of the Gestapo. A dark strand is provided by the liaison between Manfredi and Marina, a night-club performer, who has sold her soul to the Germans in return for smart clothes and for drugs – her collaboration is an addiction. Marina is in love with Manfredi who realises he must break with her but does not do so in time to escape her betrayal of him. The third story is of the love between Francesco, working as an underground printer, and Pina, a widow with a young son, Marcello. The film begins with their wedding day in the offing but the marriage is not to be: a round up of the block of flats in which Pina lives leads to the arrest of Francesco. Pina, distraught at the sight, breaks free from the German soldiers and runs after the lorry taking Francesco away. In a celebrated action sequence, we watch her being shot in the street, the camera's distance from the event matching our helplessness before it (which also cast its spell on Melville in the way he shoots the death of Mathilde). In a dramatic twist to this story, Francesco is freed from his captors in an ambush of the lorries by partisans. Later in the film, he avoids arrest by the Gestapo by sheer chance and at the end, beyond the life of the film, we assume that Pina's boy Marcello with whom Francesco has formed a bond will be looked after by him.

At the centre of this action is Don Pietro, the parish priest of the Church of St Elena in the working-class district of Rome called Praenestino.We find in the characters of the film the range of response to the occupiers: Manfredi's undiluted resistance, the cowardice of a deserter at the prospect of being tortured, the full-blooded collaboration of the Italian Chief of Police, the unthinking fraternisation with the enemy of Lauretta (Pina's sister who is described by Pina as 'stupid'), the dark collaboration of Marina that suppresses her conscience and leads, as it led Judas, to the act of betrayal. Marina is drawn with some complexity, for she loves Manfredi without understanding the danger of his situation. Her physical fatigue and degradation is a moral one as well, so that she seems to sleepwalk into giving him away. The other person in whom Rossellini and his scriptwriters invest a similar complexity is that of Don Pietro but in the opposite direction to Marina: his religion sharpens his sense of moral duty. He therefore does what he can for the Resistance in a non-violent way: he carries messages, he forges passports and he uses his church as a cover for clandestine activity. In practice he conspires with the necessary violence against the occupier, arguing that he only does this out of love for people in need: to take part is, as he says to Major Bergmann, the 'practice of charity'. This work is an extension of his ordinary priestly role: for example, trying to convince Pina about the presence of God during the occupation (she asks 'doesn't Christ see us?' to which he replies that we have so much to be pardoned for and all we can do is to pray and forgive others); and calming the deserter he shares a cell with after his arrest: 'Be calm, try to pray.' The celebrated sequence of Pina's death is concluded with a shot of Don Pietro cradling the dead victim in his arms in a modern day version of the *pietà*. Amidst so much suffering, he is the fount of compassion.

Above all, the key relationship of the film is that between Manfredi and Don Pietro. Manfredi is a Communist, arrested in 1928 for conspiring against the state and condemned to 12 years in prison. Having escaped, he rises to membership of the Committee for National Liberation. When this hard line resister first meets Don Pietro, he sets aside any antipathy in favour of forging the necessary links at the human level. Don Pietro is no different, for when Bergmann demands why he should consort with an atheist, he responds that both of them fight for justice and freedom, for 'the ways of the Lord are infinite'. This conception of God is of one who can make sense of conflicting human activity.

The final sequences of the film bring this relationship into complete focus. After his arrest, Manfredi is tortured to make him divulge his resistance contacts but both 'afraid and calm' he says nothing, the clarity of his hatred giving him the strength not to betray. Bergmann forces Don Pietro to watch and at the close of the scene blurts at him: 'Satisfied with your Christian charity?' He then lifts Manfredi's face up for Don Pietro and us to see: it is ravaged with blood and the marks of torture. Bergmann pronounces him 'your brother in Christ' as Pilate had pronounced 'ecce homo/behold the man' in John 19:5. Manfredi is dead and Don Pietro says 'it is finished', Jesus' last words on the cross in John 19:30. During Manfredi's torture his arms are pinned to the wall above his head like the crucified Jesus and it has been suggested that Rossellini has in mind a painting of the crucifixion by Renato Guttuso of 1940–1, in which the three crosses on Calvary are surrounded by distraught women and indifferent men, all naked, while in the foreground are the instruments of the Passion: knife, nails, vinegar. The presence of horses suggests the influence of Picasso's *Guernica* of 1937 on Guttuso, and both paintings order the horror of war in an expressive new way. In echoing the painting, Rossellini uses the chief tool of cinema, the supposedly objective camera, to order and direct in a similarly expressive way how the viewer should interpret the banal facts of suffering.

For the final sequence, he resorts to the prosaic: Don Pietro is taken to some open ground at the Forte Bravetta, tied in a chair and shot by firing squad. To the priest accompanying him he comments, 'it is easy to die; the difficulty is to live decently'. Rossellini deliberately films his dignified death in a matter-of-fact way. It is the torture sequence in the Gestapo HQ that he dramatises and the crucifixion is reserved for the atheist Manfredi, his death being made a symbol for the murder of justice and freedom.

It is films like Visconti's *Ossessione* and De Sica's *Bicycle Thieves* that most embody the neo-realist creed of shooting films with non-professionals in the open air. Rossellini distrusted 'neo-realist' as a label for his films, but undoubtedly the documentary quality of the exterior scenes, coupled with the subject matter, turned the film into a shot heard round the world. While Rossellini does use non-professionals in *Rome, Open City*, some of the roles being taken by friends, for the most part the film is shot indoors with trained actors in claustrophobic settings: Pina's cramped apartment, Don Pietro's vestry, the Gestapo HQ. Some of its resonance as a work of art is the way it draws on Puccini's *Tosca* (1896–9), the Italian opera mixing *verismo* with the height-ened dramatic means that belongs to music. Notably *Tosca*, like *Rome, Open City*, grounds its melodrama in the actual: the church of Sant' Andrea della Valle, the Palazzo Farnese, the Castel Sant' Angelo – church, police headquarters, prison. In Act 2 of *Tosca*, Scarpia the Chief of Police tortures Cavaradossi before Tosca's eyes in order to persuade her to divulge the whereabouts of the escaped political prisoner Angelotti. Initially we hear Cavaradossi's cries as his head suffers under the pressure of a circlet of iron. He is then brought before Tosca and the audience, bloodied but still defiant. *Rome, Open City* uses the same dramatic tension: Scarpia/Bergmann tortures Cavaradossi/Manfredi to extract information on the whereabouts of resistance fighters. Like Tosca, Don Pietro is forced to act as witness. There is a bitterness about this sequence that comes from the harrowing rawness of the memory but nods to Puccini even as it draws on the goings-on in the Gestapo HQ in the Via Tasso right up until the moment of liberation only a few months previous to its making. There is urgency among all involved to show Italians and the whole world what had happened behind closed doors, and to use the graphicness of cinema to ram the reality home.

The deserter arrested with Manfredi and Don Pietro hangs himself in his cell. Rossellini implies that it is an act of cowardice, a denial of the purpose of life which should be the courageous pursuit of justice and freedom, even if it ends with death, for death is transformed into redemptive sacrifice. Rossellini makes the point with an extraordinary dexterity. With Pina's death fresh in our minds, he shows a van being driven to a restaurant and two live sheep being taken in. Next Manfredi, Francesco and Marina meet. The proprietor brings Manfredi the news that his colleague Mazzetti has been arrested. We hear a shot, the three go to a window, and we look onto a courtyard where the two sheep are being slaughtered. Marina mutters 'poor beasts'. The iconography is exactly that of Francesco de Zurbaran's painting *The Bound Lamb*, depicting a lamb tied by the feet and lying on a stone slab. 'He was oppressed, and he was afflicted, yet he opened not his mouth: he is brought as a lamb to the slaughter, and as a sheep before her shearers is dumb.' (Isaiah 53:7–8) The bound lamb is Christ, the innocent atonement for sin. The glimpsed death of the sheep in the restaurant tells us that Mazzetti is another innocent victim, echoing the death of Pina and foreshadowing those of Manfredi who similarly 'opened not his mouth' and of Don Pietro, tied unresistingly to the chair in which he is shot.

8

Pietà

*There is something in us that can be without us and will be
after us.*

Sir Thomas Browne, *Religio Medici*, sect. 36

Death in war, like that of the gangsters described in chapter 5, is
usually instant. When depicted in the cinema, it has a shocking,
breathless quality: whether it is the casual act of violence with
gun or sword that despatches an enemy, or the extravagant
death throes filmed in slow motion so that the victim spins out
the moment. Yet a moment it remains. Even on their sickbeds,
patients dying before the camera merit only a passing mention
compared with the living. The narrative waits for no one; the
audience is likely to be impatient for the next development. It
comes as a shock therefore to watch Maurice Pialat's *La Gueule
ouverte* (*Mouth Agape*), a film he produced, wrote and directed
himself, which gives it a very personal, possibly autobiographical
feel. Its narrative is of the simplest. It starts with a woman called
Monique being X-rayed for signs of cancer and ends with her
death and funeral. It is not clear whether her death takes weeks
or months but we are shown her progressive deterioration from
suspect health to her horizontal end, without voice, without
response. Because her son, Philippe, is looking after her at the
beginning, we think that the film is going to be about the rela-

tionship between them, with a role for his wife Nathalie. But when the doctors tell Philippe that there is nothing more that they can do and ask whether she can be looked after at home, she is taken to her native Auvergne to be cared for by her husband Roger, who runs a clothes shop 'La Maison de la Laine'. The film then widens into a study of this triangle, how the husband/father, wife/mother and son respond to each other. Furthermore, it turns out that the film is as much about sex as death. We learn at the very beginning that Roger has been unfaithful to Monique all through his life, so much so that his promiscuity has earned him the nickname of 'The Satyr'. Nor, despite his age, does his carnal appetite seem hugely diminished. In any case it lives on in Philippe, who while keeping his marriage alive, engages in casual sex with other women. For the wives, Monique and Nathalie, this is the subject of complaint but they do not allow it to affect the status of their marriage.

The family sounds dysfunctional but one of Pialat's purposes is to show how humans care for each other. Roger and Philippe are exemplary in their attention to Monique, visiting her in hospital, sitting with her as she lies mutely in her sickbed at home, patiently feeding her, listening to her raving as her mind deteriorates, and finally watching her slip away. Another preoccupation is to present life as ritualistic, as if humans live their lives going through the motions: the routines of the hospital, visiting twice a day, picking up a prostitute, serving a customer, watching the patient die. This being a French film, cigarettes are a routine solace and indeed smoking and sexual intercourse exist on the same plane: it is what you engage in when you want something to fill a gap. Another option in modern society is to turn on the television but there is a subtle shade given to Roger's character, an echo of older mores: when his son flicks a switch 'just to watch the news', Roger forbids it exclaiming, 'Have you no respect?' The film climaxes in the singular ritual that happens to those who die in bed at home. We see nurses strip Monique of her nightdress and then, having gazed at her naked body in which rigor mortis is beginning to freeze her horizontality, we watch with Roger and Philippe as her body is wrapped in a shroud and coffined. The funeral is well attended, for death in a small town is a community affair. It is encompassed in a single shot: the camera tracks forward slowly along the church wall toward a row of sober and impassive spectators, then coming to the corner it pans slowly right to reveal Philippe and Nathalie by the hearse in the middle distance, only Nathalie betraying a modest restlessness. Until Monique is buried, statuesque waiting remains part of the ritual. The church is at the margins, to be imagined, if imagined at all, virtually off the screen. Pialat proceeds by hints: earlier in the film we see through a window, therefore darkly as it were, as Roger talks to the parish priest in ill-fitting cassock, but hear only the fag-end (appropriate in Roger's case) of the conversation when the priest tells Roger, 'The church is much maligned.' A friction is only sketched. Similarly when the dead Monique is stripped, there is a brief still life of a crucifix lying on the bed, revealed at the end, a secret rather than a public comfort.

This quality of observation inherent in the style of the film renders the spectator powerless. But into this barren void Pialat unleashes something ambiguous that can begin to connect us. In showing Roger's devotion to the dying Monique he invites us to see it almost as automatic. However, when she is coffined, Roger breaks down in a paroxysm of grief, desperate not to let her go. Philippe then embraces his father in compassion and as spectators we suddenly experience real emotion breaking through. Yet the film ends unresolved: is this weeping merely another ritual? Right at the end, after the burial, Philippe and Nathalie protest that Roger should not remain in the 'Maison de la Laine' on his own because he should not be alone but come with them. Roger is obstinate, insisting he must 'stay with her', as if her soul is appeased only in company. Philippe and Nathalie, having offered their dutiful comfort, get into the car and drive off; the camera, watching out of the back window, tracks away from the shop, past the church, down the street and then the tree-lined road, leaving the town as if forever: the process of forgetting has already begun. In the final shot, Roger turns out the lights in the shop and the screen goes black.

Like music, film is linear: the spectator is taken on a straight line through time, allowed neither to turn back and dwell on a previous scene, nor to skip forward. *Mouth Agape* has a detachment but the progression of Monique's disease gives the story a decelerated urgency. In a sequence lasting seven minutes, her end is recorded. Nothing is said; the only sound is her breathing. Philippe is watching his mother in medium shot, Roger enters, they both watch, Roger leaves and then returns, then leaves. Cut to the exterior of the shop, lit at night, marking a passage of time. Cut to the bedroom: Roger massages Monique's feet, then leaves, while for over 20 seconds the camera lingers on her, wheezing rather than breathing, or breathing as sighing. Cut to Roger in his own room blowing his nose in anticipation at the paroxysm to come. Cut to Philippe in his room reading. Cut to the corridor: the father calls to his son, 'C'est fini/It's all over.' They come into the room together to look at the dead body.

In spite of our impatient world, people continue to die slowly. The film seems to be old-fashioned in asserting this truth. Its tone echoes Ecclesiastes, 'There is a time to live and a time to die . . . All is vanity.' Creation continues in a revolving world; the life and death of humans is only a small part and it makes no difference whether you believe God fashioned the world or not. Yet compassion can give meaning. When Roger breaks down and Philippe embraces his father, *Mouth Agape* bursts its self-made prison. In *Mother and Son* the Russian Aleksandr Sokurov takes this explosion of feeling and uses it to suggest the beauty and abundance of God's creation. The story is even simpler: on the last day of her life, a dying mother is cared for by her son in the depths of the Russian countryside. He carries her outside; they rest in the fields; he carries her back in; he goes for a second walk and returns to find her dead. All this lasts 73 minutes. Its greatness as a film is in the way Sokurov leads us from intensity to intensity. The son's attention to his mother is devotional. 'Pietà' is Italian for 'mercy' and is also used to describe the image of Mary the mother cradling the dead Jesus, her son. Sokurov inverts the relationship: the son cradles the mother, so that he might carry her frail shrunken body through the fields one last time. When they pause at the edge of the field, she sleeps then wakes and asks him to tell her something. He recites some shared memory and then breaks off. In the ensuing silence he comments, 'God's creation, how beautiful.' He is describing the landscape before him, but he is also describing the inner landscape of their relationship. Pialat's *Mouth Agape* does not deny God so much as suggest that his presence is unknowable. In *Mother and Son* on the other hand Sokurov, the Russian Romantic, sees each action, each word, the whole world as revealing some supernatural beauty breaking through, as revealing the immanence of the divine. Is there some special 'Russian' quality here? This attraction to showing visual surface is a long way from Bergman's version of Protestantism, to take one extreme, but shared with Andrei Tarkovsky, master of the gaze lingering on the world.

Sokurov gives the film intensity by the reverence he bestows on two people's actions. But he doubles this by a very bold stylistic effect: the cameraman Aleksei Fyodorov used painted screens, filters and mirrors to approximate the image to painting, a far step from Maurice Pialat's plain photography. Sokurov has stated that his starting-point was a painting of 1810 by Caspar David Friedrich, *The Monk by the Sea*, and he sought to recreate in the mood of the film 'the dramatic atmosphere of paintings like that'. As important as giving the film a painterly surface is the use of refracted light to elongate faces and landscapes. Sometimes mother and son seem to lean into each other, at other times they lean away. Their features are not distorted but blurred and softened. Sokurov chooses also to shoot on a telephoto lens that reduces the distance between figures and background. All these techniques reduce spatial sense and enhance the image as surface. So often the cinema aims to create reality through illusion; here Sokurov deliberately creates illusion.

There are some 60 shots in the film, giving an average shot length for the whole of over a minute. Such deceleration is strange to us, almost disturbing, yet utterly appropriate to a film about the process of death. The sequences of inaction are punctuated by Friedrich-like images of isolation including the wind moving in a field of grass, and a schooner far at sea working slowly towards the edge of the frame. Most notably, a distant train travels through the fields, the steam from its funnel making a clear white vapour trail tearing the green in half. Although the film is scattered with dialogue and the quality of the images binds the whole together, it is in the soundtrack that creation makes itself most intensely felt. Although we see the train we more often hear its whistle, like the cry of an upland bird, more heard than seen. Because it is spring, there is also birdsong; in the house a fly buzzes. We see crows flapping above pines but it is their cawing that arrests us. Bells are heard. There are dim snatches of music, symphonic and pianistic, reinforcing the film's nineteenth-century quality. Most persistently, thunder, that harbinger of changing weather or season, rumbles through the film from the sky darkened by Fyodorov's filters. Friedrich's paintings of man alone in the landscape before the beauty, or rather the awesomeness of creation, have been realised on film, only this time the subject pierces the ear as well as the eye. The cinema is revealed as having the potential to enlarge the experience we derive from looking at paintings.

We barely identify with the mother and the son since we are told too little to unravel their personal histories. The film seeks instead to create wonder. The nearest it gets to dénouement is at the end when the son returns to find his mother dead and gives an anguished cry. In a final *coup de cinéma* Sokurov uses the image of a just-alive butterfly on her hand to proclaim the fragility of creation both human and animal. We leave the film with its mood resonating in the head. This is a mental more than an emotional experience and all the more persistent for that.

Mother and Son is breaking down the walls within which we watch films. It is marvellous on the large cinema screen, but it is also intensely experienced on video, where the privacy of our watching can be unaffected by any sense of impatience in the audience. It is video technology of a public kind that offers us another sight of death. Bill Viola's tape installation of 1992, *The Nantes Triptych*, is both public and private. Installed in a dark gallery rather than the cinema, it is seen by spectators coming and going as they wish, while the video tape runs things happening in real time uninterrupted by edits. We can share with Roger and Philippe the act of watching someone die. Viola's triptych is on three screens in conscious homage to Renaissance churches the frescoes of which are, in his words, 'a form of installation, a physical, spatial, consuming experience'. On the left screen a young woman is in the final stages of labour, culminating in the birth of her baby. In the middle a figure moves about underwater, described by Viola as a form of self-portrait 'floating in another world with the experience of life and death'. For, on the right-hand side, the tape shows Viola's mother in her final illness. Like Pialat's Monique and Sokurov's Mother her face is pale and ghostly, marked with suffering but in her final moments fully engaging the attention of her son operating the video camera. In this case our vision is enlarged: death is balanced by birth. The two images do not conflict but merge into a total experience of the preciousness of life, to which both events are central, not just objectively but to the subjective individual who links the two. Joy at watching a child being born and compassion at the sight of an old woman dying are two sides of one coin: both break open our propensity for wonder, and wonder breaks open love.

9

Crucifixion

There isn't a kingdom of the living and a kingdom of the dead. There's a kingdom of God and we are in it.

Georges Bernanos

Mother and Son comes close to showing death as the release of the soul, a belief prevalent in medieval times. When her persecutors sent Joan of Arc to be burnt at the stake, they used the cruellest form of execution, since not just the body but the soul as well was thought to be consumed in the conflagration. When he filmed *Le Procès de Jeanne d'Arc* (*The Trial of Joan of Arc*) in 1961, Robert Bresson made a point of ending the film with the image of the stump to which Joan's burnt body had been tied. It is charred and smoking, and suggests her presence beyond the destruction of her corporeal existence.

Filming Joan's martyrdom presents a challenge common to all films about the past. If we want to film something set in the fifteenth century, 600 years ago, how can we know what people wore, how they cut their hair, how much furniture they had, what the surface of walls looked like, what were the fashionable mannerisms of the time? Literature gives us some clues and there is some visual evidence in pictures and in archaeological remains, yet they remain clues not full answers. To a film-maker with a scrupulous notion of what is real, these questions are not negligible ones. The Dane, Carl Theodor Dreyer, was such a person, with claims on being the most singular film-making talent to have emerged from twentieth-century cinema. There are several grounds for this, one of which is the way he solved the problem of creating a persuasive historical setting for his films. The challenge involved did not deter him from choosing stories set in the historical past, but he evolved a deliberate strategy of simplification, 'purification' as he called it, to create rooms and clothes of some historical verisimilitude that would help the actors settle in to their roles, on the grounds that if the actors have a conviction about the spaces in which they move and the clothes they wear, then the audience can be convinced as well. This approach underpins Dreyer's special gift for direct-ing actors and actresses, in particular the latter since his films often have a female protagonist at their centre.

La Passion de Jeanne d'Arc (*The Passion of Joan of Arc*), which he filmed in 1927, is the only silent film discussed in this book. Unusually, even for its time, it is a true silent. It was very much the practice in the years before the advent of synchronised dia-logue around 1927 for films to be accompanied by a keyboard player or an orchestra. Dreyer seems to have conceived his film to be shown without musical accompaniment and when the film was restored and released again in 1985, based on a rediscovered original negative, it was done without a musical soundtrack. This makes the experience of viewing the film one to which we are quite unaccustomed, indeed it is almost revolutionary, for we have no aural element to fall back on that might tide us over the passages where we lose concentration. To make matters harder, Dreyer insists on concentration in his spectator, for he has sought it and achieved it in his actors, especially Marie Falconetti playing Joan. In 1965 he said in an interview:

> With Falconetti it was very often the case that after working all afternoon, we had failed to reach exactly what was wanted. We said to ourselves, we shall start again tomorrow. The next day, we projected the unsatisfactory take of the

day before, studied it, probed it, and always concluded by finding in it some small fragments, some hints which reproduced precisely the expression, the tonality we had been looking for. So we started again from there, taking the best and dropping the remainder, using it to start again . . . and succeeding.

Since the film was shot over six months, which is a long shooting schedule, Dreyer reveals in this description the immense demands made on Falconetti to reach the result he wanted.

So, after the sets and costumes were carefully created, after the actors were pushed to their limits, there remained the third key question for Dreyer: what to do with the camera? Again, his strategy was an exceptional one. Where directors use close-ups on faces, they do so sparingly in order to dramatise a particular moment. For *Joan of Arc*, Dreyer used close-ups as the norm, dispensing with make-up at the same time, as if seeking to penetrate beyond the pores of the skin, beyond the mask of human expression, into the inner nature of his characters. By the end of the film, Falconetti's face has begun to haunt us: its roundness, the big trembling lips, and above all her large round eyes, never blinking. This is a face a portrait painter could make much of but would have to distil all its character into a single configuration. The cinema brings something new to human representation: the possibility of coming into intimate contact with a person's face in constant metamorphosis. We observe, literally face to face, all her transient reactions, brought to light by the camera's single-minded gaze. The effect of her ordeal on Joan is given the starkest, most emotional expression possible. Fear is visible from timidity to terror. Shame is visible from confusion to pleading. Resignation is visible from bafflement to acceptance. Joy is visible from illumination to transfiguration. When Joan weeps, as she does frequently in the film, her tears are the most celebrated in the history of film. After she has signed the abjuration her judges desire, and has been condemned to life imprisonment, Dreyer shows hair clippings on the floor. He then shows her head being shaved: for a woman a signal humiliation. Joan weeps. A contemporary account of the filming tells how this scene was filmed in silence: 'Our sensibilities were stirred as if this badge of infamy was being applied to her in real life. The electricians and the technicians held their breath, and their eyes filled with tears.' Falconetti wept for the camera and at the end Dreyer went gently up to her 'collected one of her tears in his fingers and brought it to his lips'.

The expressivity of Dreyer's close-ups distilled film acting to perfection. The early silent cinema captured a strongly gestural style derived from the theatre of the day, with facial expressions to match. On the eve of the arrival of the sound film, which would change everything, Dreyer arrived at a style that was emotional, but nuanced for the camera only a few feet away rather than for an audience at the back of a theatre, making the raising of an eyebrow into a violent gesture. The intimacy of the procedure is symbolised by one particular moment: Joan is trapped by her inquisitors into a position near to admitting she has no need of the Church. In her confusion as to how to reply she puts her hand to her mouth in anxiety. We are close enough to see a fly alight on her forehead. She brushes it off lightly, while retaining her look of perplexity, in an unrehearsed gesture showing her inner doubt.

The style is in stark contrast to Bresson's version of 34 years later. It is his most static, wordy film and the camera studiously keeps the figures in the middle distance, close-ups being reserved for the shackles on Joan's feet. Bresson's film is almost a critique of Dreyer's, as if made with a polemical intent, namely to accuse the expressivity in the earlier film of falseness and to deny that the soul of the character is visible through the face of an actress. Instead it is only revealed through the mechanical style of a non-professional (as miraculously achieved in *Pickpocket*).

Both film-makers have used the minutes of the trial preserved in the Bibliothèque Nationale in Paris. In fact Dreyer wanted to make a talking film but had to abandon the idea because the French studios did not have the necessary equipment. The intertitles giving the blunt questions of Joan's accusers and her simple replies were important to Dreyer, who wanted them embedded in the surrounding visual material, although they do break up the superlative visual rhythm of the film. Bresson has the advantage of sound technology, but in the end it is surely Dreyer rather than Bresson who has made the masterpiece. Bresson was focussed on the legal intricacies of the trial, the verbal battle between accusers and accused. Dreyer was likewise drawn to this, but his finished result is something more, an expression of the ordeal Joan underwent, a woman before men, a young woman before elders, innocence before experience. It is not for nothing that the film is titled *The **Passion** of Joan of Arc*, for if there are any forerunners to Dreyer's work it is the tradition evolved by Renaissance painting in Northern Europe of depicting the trial and crucifixion of Jesus. He is a victim before ugly and cruel humanity, and his body and face bear the marks of physical and mental torture. Dreyer makes the parallel explicit in the sequence when three English soldiers, who set a crown of rope on her head and place an arrow in her hand as a sceptre, laughing and leering as they do so, make a mockery of Joan. She makes no resistance, her distress being signalled by a tear welling from her eye. As we saw in chapter 7, Rossellini had made use of the symbolism of the bound lamb in *Rome, Open City*. Dreyer has the same passage of Isaiah (53:7–8) in mind but uses it literally rather than symbolically. The lamb being prepared for sacrifice is taken in the Christian tradition as a prophecy of the nature and meaning of Christ's passion: the man of sorrows 'brought as a lamb to the slaughter. And as a sheep before her shearers is dumb, so he openeth not his mouth.' Thus Joan undergoes the shearing of the locks from her head, without complaint or resistance.

However, it is also the case that, unlike for example Grünewald's *Crucifixion* of the early sixteenth century (in the Basel Kunstmuseum), Dreyer eschews the grotesque. Joan was tortured during her trial and in the film she is brought into the torture chamber to be confronted by the medieval machinery of pain. Dreyer intercuts the spinning of a spiked wheel with Joan's growing terror. She faints. The loss of consciousness is induced not by physical punishment, but the prospect of it. This delicacy preserves Joan's spiritual aura in the film rather than traducing it with physical scars.

Joan of Arc has been called Dreyer's 'avant-garde' film and it can well take its place among the boldest and most enduring products of the flowering of the cinema in the 1920s. Its radicalism, like that of Sokurov's *Mother and Son*, can be measured in the shot lengths, but whereas Sokurov used only 60 shots, Dreyer, albeit in a longer film, uses some 800 to 850. Towards the end, the pace of the editing, uninterrupted by intertitles and intercutting the burning Joan, the flaming logs, the angry crowd and the violent soldiers, becomes frenetic, like a symphony moving into a higher gear. On the other hand Dreyer was a classical director who was concerned in his later films with a natural acting style, who ensured his sets exhibited a classical restraint, who like a theatre dramatist regarded dramatic structure as a key to the narrative film. *Joan of Arc* therefore observes strong unity of time and place, the trial of three months being distilled into a single day. Settings are the courtroom, Joan's cell, the torture chamber and the cobbled market place, all apparently adjacent to one another. A further unity is supplied by the fact that the white walls of the castle rooms (painted pink so that they glowed when filmed in black and white) match the white sky of the final exterior sequence, making the move from inside to outside a seamless one.

The 92-minute film can be broken down into sections, as follows:

1. Courtroom: Joan before Bishop Cauchon, the presiding judge, and the priests and soldiers (18 minutes). A judge concludes by telling the English sergeant: 'We must resort to subterfuge.'
2. Joan's cell: a letter from King Charles is forged urging Joan to trust one of the priests. He then leads her into a trap during

the interrogation. Cauchon concludes that she is a fiend of Satan and orders torture to be prepared (16 minutes).

3. In an interlude Joan is mocked by English soldiers and rescued by a priest appointed to defend her (4 minutes).
4. The torture chamber: Joan refuses to recant and faints (7 minutes).
5. Joan's cell: she is bled, and the sacrament is prepared, but when Joan refuses to sign the abjuration it is denied to her (11 minutes).
6. The market place: the trial continues before a crowd of spectators, and Joan finally signs the paper of abjuration. A commotion begins among the crowd in reaction to the sentence of life imprisonment (10 minutes).
7. Joan's cell: her head is shaved. She recants her signing of the abjuration (6 minutes).
8. Joan's cell, then market place: Joan is prepared for death with the sacrament of Holy Communion, intercut with continued crowd restlessness. She is led into the market place and burnt at the stake. The film ends with the soldiers suppressing a full-scale riot (20 minutes).

The film seems to have been conceived initially as an account of Joan's trial. Pierre Champion, whose edition of the proceedings of the trial of condemnation had been published in 1920-1, is listed as historical adviser. But the result is something much larger, a paradigmatic representation of martyrdom, a revelation of how plain narrative can be transformed into an essential story in our lives. In the Christian tradition martyrdom is expressed in passive but steadfast opposition to authority in murderous mood. Its essence is the use of powerlessness to bring the bystander to your side, and in the end to overwhelm your enemy. Its weapons are not physical but supernatural. Its inspiration is Christ before his captors. The choice for the martyr is death and glory or compromise and failure: salvation is in death not life. For all its realism, *Joan of Arc* is less a courtroom drama than a celebration of Saint Joan, who had been canonised by the Catholic Church only a few years earlier.

We think of martyrdom as something historical, belonging to the early life of the church, or the struggle between Protestantism and Catholicism during the Reformation and Counter-Reformation. Yet the resonance of Dreyer's film in the modern age is enormous and has only been appreciated in the fullness of time. Among the inspirations for the film is Eisenstein's *Battleship Potemkin*, which had taken European film societies by storm in the mid-1920s. It is the celebrated massacre on the Odessa steps, the dramatic hinge of *Potemkin*, which had surely led Dreyer to end *Joan of Arc* not just with her immolation but with the repression of the riot that accompanies it. The sequence in *Potemkin* is famous both for Eisenstein's use of montage, building a total effect that far outstrips the sum of the short fragments that make it up, and for its violence. Even after a century of screen bloodshed, this Tsarist suppression of a peaceful demonstration remains graphic. Its cruelty is distilled in a Marxist version of the *pietà*: a proletarian mother carrying her dead son stands screaming before a row of soldiers, the shock troops of the ruling class. In *Joan of Arc* the restless crowd are mostly women and the soldiers are English, wielding spears and spiked metal balls, even firing a cannon into the defenceless crowd. Near the end, a child weeps over its mother lying dead on the cobbles.

Just as Eisenstein, in obedience to Marxist-Leninist principles, turns the events of 1905, a failed revolution, into the foundations of the successful one in 1917, so Dreyer is proclaiming Joan's death as the triumph of spirit over the grave, of the individual over authority. With the collapse of Communism Eisenstein's myth now feels like a tract, but we are still absorbing Dreyer's polemic against intolerance toward the individual conscience, especially as wielded by men against women. Six hundred years on, the portrayal of villainous religious authority caused the Archbishop of Paris to insist on a censored version before its release in 1928. Its potency is even greater than that: it was not for nothing that the film was banned in occupied Europe during the Second World War.

Nor does its currency as a work of art end there. Joan's fiery faith in God is true to the Middle Ages but it is also a challenge to an age of doubt. We suffer from a loss of self-confidence, we relish the triumph of ironic narrative, we are uncertain of whether we have a purpose on earth: Dreyer's portrayal of Joan gives us an uncompromising parable about unalloyed faith, a theme to which he was to return in *The Word*.

10

Resurrections

For this corruptible must put on incorruption, and this mortal must put on immortality.

Paul, 1 Corinthians 15:53

Visual art can bring us sight of the body raised from the dead, making credible the extraordinary fact beyond the power of words in a novel. Given the dramatic power of the idea, it is surprising that the dead coming back to life has not been more widely used in painting (although Piero della Francesca's powerful picture of the risen Christ stepping from the tomb comes to mind), so when the Danish pastor and playwright, Kaj Munk, wrote his play *Ordet* (*The Word*) in the early 1930s about a dead woman being brought back to life, he seemed to be entering new territory. As it turns out, he did have a starting-point: the Norwegian playwright Bjørnson had written *Beyond Our Power* about the miraculous healing of an incurable. This gave Munk an insight into the miracle as a dramatic idea, and he combined this with the idea of resurrection, for which there was a direct narrative precedent, the gospel account of Jesus' raising of Lazarus (John 11:1–43). This story had so stirred the Danish metaphysician, Søren Kierkegaard, that he made it central in his philosophy, the miracle among miracles. Christian faith, he proposed, is unlike all accepted forms of human cognition, for it is in itself miraculous, flying in the face of all that we know in the scientific sense about the world.

When Carl Dreyer saw Munk's play on its first appearance, not long after completing *Joan of Arc*, he was 'overcome with admiration for the apparent ease with which the writer presented his paradoxical assertions'. There is a hint here that he may have been struck by its absurdity as much as by its power. It may also be that he found in the story of *The Word* an echo of the film he had made in 1925 called *Master of the House*. This is a domestic comedy about a husband, Victor, who tyrannises his wife Ida until the old family nanny, sick of his behaviour, contrives to send Ida away and in her absence teach Victor the value of all his wife does for him. Chastened, he longs for her return, which is stage managed by the nanny as an unexpected, almost miraculous reappearance. The story is another of Dreyer's assaults on patriarchy but he makes Ida's return into a revelation of love. It was this idea, as well as that of physical resurrection, that stirred Dreyer in *The Word* and when he made the film of Munk's play twenty years later, he reused an idea from *Master of the House* to signal the link between the two: after the revelation/resurrection takes place in each film, the pendulum clock on the wall, halted to mark the moment of loss, is restarted as a sign of life beginning again, the fullness of living only being made possible by the presence of feminine loving.

By 1944 Kaj Munk had been martyred at the hands of the Gestapo, in reprisal for his travelling across Denmark giving public witness from the pulpit to the tyranny of Nazism. Now Dreyer was greatly attracted to the idea of the individual stubbornly holding to a view in defiance of authority, hence his *Joan of Arc*; hence his interest in Munk as a person; hence his interest in the character of Johannes at the centre of Munk's play. *The Word* was filmed ten years after Munk's death and is an act of homage as well as being a remarkable film. The comedy of domestic manners he had made in 1925 becomes a sombre meditation on loss and the conquest of suffering. The resurrection of Inger by her brother-in-law Johannes forms its climax. Dressed

in white, her corpse is laid in a coffin in the parlour of
Borgensgaard, the home of her father-in-law Morten Borgen and
his family. Behind her, the transparent curtains filter the light.
The resulting whiteness of the room is the frame in which the
characters move, all dressed in black. Unexpectedly, Johannes
Borgen, Morten's son, enters. Having studied for the priesthood,
Johannes has never completed his preparation and in the eyes of
his family has become unhinged, uttering sombre but meaningless prophecies. (Too much study, especially of Kierkegaard, is
cited as the cause.) When Inger dies, he goes missing and all
attempts to find him fail. His entry into the room is therefore a
coup de théâtre. What is more he seems to his family, and to us as
spectators, in his right mind. Going to the coffin and encouraged by Inger's little girl, the only member of the family to take
him seriously, he commands Inger to rise up. She wakes, sits up
and throws her arms round her husband Mikkel.

Described on its own this final scene seems ridiculous. Yet the
core of the film's power is in making it a dramatic conclusion to
a tragic story, just as Lazarus' resurrection is, and just as in the
gospel, the resurrection of Jesus makes no particular sense except
in the context of the whole narrative. In the Borgen home, Inger
is the woman whose warmth and love cements the whole family,
who has done everything except produce a male heir. At the
beginning she is pregnant and old Morten hopes for a boy. In
the event, the baby is stillborn; then, to add to the family's suffering, Inger dies as well. Her resurrection is miraculous but a
longed-for outcome to the story.

It is against this backdrop that Johannes' adoption of the
persona of Christ seems so unbalanced. He appears mentally
beyond rescue and in a sane person his words would seem
terrifyingly harsh. While Morten waits in the parlour for the outcome of Inger's labour, Johannes proclaims a vision of the man
with 'the hourglass and the scythe', come first for the child, then
for Inger herself. This produces an angry reaction in Morten,
who shouts, 'Will you be quiet?' Our sympathies are with the
broken old man but the film turns them on their head. As it

turns out, Morten is 'living under the law', by the Old Testament as it were, while many of Johannes' words quote the New, and it is by the miracle of the raising of Inger that the Borgen world is made whole again, prompting Morten to recognise in the deed the hand of the God of Elijah, who had raised the child of the widow of Zarephath (1 Kings 17:17–24) 'eternal and the same'. At first the film leads us into the territory of Dostoevsky's parable of the Grand Inquisitor in *The Brothers Karamazov*. Halfway through the film Johannes encounters the new pastor come to visit, who doubts, not unreasonably, Johannes' assertion that he is Jesus of Nazareth. To the pastor's statement that miracles no longer happen Johannes replies: 'Thus speaks my church on earth . . . Here I stand and again you cast me out. But if you nail me to the cross a second time, woe unto you.' It is the act of raising the dead that leads us out of this metaphysical cul-de-sac. Baldly explained, it seems supernatural, but Munk/Dreyer do two things to deter that conclusion. Firstly, the character of Johannes is consistent, deeds follow his words; second, Dreyer's loving care in the creation of the interiors and in using the landscape of sand, grass and reed gives the film a realistic feel. We take it as natural that the unbalanced Johannes, kept at home by Morten out of family love rather than being put in an institution, has a place among the living and that his insanity may in the end make him into a worker of miracles.

The Word is set in Jutland, where Denmark sticks out into the Baltic, a landscape of dunes, heaths and wide skies, between the Skagerrak and the Kattegat. There the Lutheranism of northern Europe flourished as a means of sustaining the communities toiling for a living from the sea or on indifferent soils, but in the narrow confines of a world at the edge of the world it also shrunk. Its legacy for Dreyer was both one of admiration at the way it fostered human life and of revulsion at the way it could produce an intolerance of the most terrifying kind (in *Day of Wrath*, which he made in 1943, any woman daring to go outside the rules is accused of witchcraft). There is a loveliness about *The Word* in the way it seeks to explode that world, not in an act that sweeps it all away, but in one that takes its essence, faith in God, and carries it to a new level beyond conventional imagination.

Babette's Gæstebud (*Babette's Feast*, 1987) is another such film. Made by Gabriel Axel, it derives from a short story by Karen Blixen written in 1950, between Munk's play and Dreyer's film, and comes out of the same world, even though it is set in the nineteenth century. This is well before the actual time of *The Word*, which in truth has a certain timelessness about it: it is the doctor's car which gives away the fact that we are in the twentieth century, that and the disbelief in miracles.

Both narratives are fables with a purpose well beyond that of merely telling a good story. They have a moral about how we should view the world. They appear to be rooted in the real, and they certainly respect the appearances of the world they depict, Axel like Dreyer taking great care in the ordering of his interiors. The film starts with two spinsters, Martina (after Martin Luther) and Philippa (after Philip Melanchthon), distributing soup and comforts to the old men of the village where they live, by the Jutland shore. They are spinsters and form lynchpins of a shrinking religious congregation that had been established by their father, a 'priest and prophet' (shades of *The Apostle* – see chapter 4). They have a French servant who is introduced coyly to us by two shots from the rear before we see her face to face and her bewitching smile. Our curiosity is aroused as to how this ménage came about and in answer to it, we are shown a flashback to the two sisters' youth when as beautiful young women in the company of their father, they were diverted by him from any prospects of marriage. In two skilful vignettes, Axel shows Martina bowling over Lorens Lowenhielm, a young officer exiled by his father to this remote area for misbehaviour; following that the famous opera singer, Achille Papin, yearning for solitude and ending up in Jutland, discovers Philippa's voice and resolves to make her the queen of the Paris opera. Both stirrings come to nothing: the sisters cannot move from their father, from each other, and from the world they know. Lowenhielm and Papin depart empty-handed.

The film then moves forward in time. Philippa and Martina still live together but without their father. On a stormy night a figure appears at the door: Babette Hersant is a Frenchwoman on the run, whose husband and son have been shot during the suppression of the Paris Commune, and who has been given the names of the sisters by an elderly Achille Papin in Paris. She is taken in as their servant and cook, and we learn casually that her only connection with Paris is the lottery ticket renewed for her each year. There she stays, while the sisters' little sect continues to shrink and become more quarrelsome. Fourteen years later, at the same time as Philippa and Martina announce a special meal to mark the hundredth anniversary of the birth of their father, Babette learns she has won 10,000 francs in the lottery. The sisters expect her to leave but instead she asks a favour, namely to prepare 'a real French dinner' for the anniversary meal. This offer is gratefully accepted but when she sets about it, bringing ashore a cargo of goods purchased far afield, including quails and a turtle, Philippa and Martina begin to take alarm. When they take their fears of a 'witches' Sabbath' to the congregation, they all resolve collectively not to enjoy the meal, to ignore it as it were.

The day arrives, but just before it, news comes that Martina's suitor in her youth, Lorens Lowenhielm, now a general, is staying with his aunt and is to accompany her to the meal. They are now twelve for supper and the guests arrive in a high wind blowing around the village street. The meal is served, with the guests reaffirming their pledge: 'Like at the wedding of Cana, the food is of no importance.' The menu is as follows:

Turtle soup – Amontillado sherry
Blinis Demidoff – Veuve Clicquot 1860
Quails 'en sarcophage' – Clos de Vougeot 1845 (i.e. a *grand cru* red burgundy of some 40 years' vintage, since the meal takes place in 1885)
Cheese
Dessert

Fresh figs
Vieux marc fine champagne
Coffee

At this unexpected abundance Lowenhielm is moved to make a speech – or rather a sermon – on the text from Psalm 85: 'Mercy and truth are met together; righteousness and peace have kissed each other.' The stoniness of the guests is melted; reconciliations are affected. Lorens speaks to Martina of the union of souls and departs. The guests emerge to a quiet starlit night, dance round the village well, and they too disperse. The sisters return to the kitchen to thank Babette who sits philosophically among the remains of the evening. They are then astounded to learn that the meal has cost all her lottery winnings of 10,000 francs, the price of a meal at the Café Anglais in Paris where she had once been chef. She is penniless again. Philippa has the final word: 'In paradise you will be the great artist.'

Axel's style is straightforward and by the 1980s he has the benefit of drawing on a distinguished tradition of Scandinavian film-making's fascination with light and dark. Made in colour, *Babette's Feast* has transmuted the blacks, whites and greys of Dreyer's and Bergman's world into browns, greens and blue-greys. *The Word* provides a ghostly presence in the persons of Birgitte Federspiel, the beautiful Inger of *The Word*, now the kindly and elderly Martina, and Preben Lerdorff Rye, the Christ-like Johannes, now a retired sea captain and member of the sect. Axel honours Bergman by casting a seasoned member of the latter's acting ensemble, Jarl Kulle, as the elderly General Lowenhielm. Inserting his monocle, he studies himself in the mirror and quotes from Ecclesiastes: 'Vanity, vanity, all is vanity.' He is a grown-up version of the Count Malcolm he plays in Bergman's *Smiles of a Summer Night* of 30 years earlier, stiff, military, monocled. Kulle brings a sense of artistic tradition to Axel's film, just as Lowenhielm brings a wider world into the remote community, just as Babette Hersant links it to revolutionary European politics, just as champagne seems to be some exotic 'lemonade' to villagers who have never tasted it before. Axel is faithful to Karen Blixen's aristocratic emphasis as a writer on hierarchy and social order. The story is a celebration of such order, seeking paradise not in its overthrow but in its fulfilment. There is a key idea of the way in which a cleavage in the human mind, most obviously in that between the material and the spiritual world, can be healed. It manifests itself in several other means: the way those who eat ale-bread soup and those who eat a meal at the Café Anglais can be brought together; the way a small sect is reunited with European civilisation; the way a feast transmutes the failed physical union between Martina and Lorens into a union of souls. When Lorens had first met Martina, he had had a vision of 'a purer life with an angel at his side', but since marriage was not to be, he has spent his career thinking of Martina (and, as it turns out, she of him) and after the meal the pain of this memory is changed. As he departs, he says to her, 'Every evening I shall sit down to dine with you, not with my body which is of no importance but with my soul.' For this scene there is a brilliant musical touch. The congregation's favourite hymn is 'Jerusalem my heart's true home', their own expression of yearning for paradise, and we see them singing it on several occasions. When at the meal Lorens and Martina silently toast each other across the table to show that they have their own shared vision of Jerusalem, the composer Per Nørgård creates from the hymn tune a dissonant version for piano, which both links them to the sect and at the same time isolates them from it.

In general, Axel has faithfully served a powerfully simple story and has a fine sense of its ironies. He shows the great French chef being given a lesson by Martina and Philippa in how to cook ale-bread soup. We learn from Papin when he sends Babette to Jutland that General Galliflet has destroyed her family in the bloody suppression of the Paris Commune. It is this same general that General Lowenhielm quotes in recalling a meal at the Café Anglais and its female chef: 'A dinner was turned into a love affair that made no distinction between bodily and spiritual appetite,' showing both generals blissfully unaware of the destruction one of them will wreak on this great chef's life. This leads into the central idea of the story, namely that Babette turns her exile into sacrifice by devoting herself to the service of the two sisters, and into a generosity beyond reason: the expenditure of 10,000 francs on one meal echoes the woman at Bethany who pours a bottle of perfume over Jesus, while the disciples are indignant at the waste of money (Matthew 26:6–13). Out of sacrifice and generosity springs reconciliation. Her meal is certainly a celebration of French cuisine, but much more than that, it is a sacramental moment celebrating the abundance of this world and conquering the yearnings of all the other characters for a better world elsewhere. That twelve sit down for a meal, that red wine is at its heart, that the old woman who has never tasted wine before rejects her glass of water in favour of a great Burgundy, points to a 'thirst for the true vine' which gives everlasting life. All bring into focus the eucharistic quality of the feast, a blessing of the present moment. The reference to the wedding at Cana is specific: water has been turned into Clos de Vougeot 1845, a miracle if not on a par with the raising of the dead, yet a miracle all the same.

In its subtle way, *Babette's Feast* puts in question the patriarchal society in which the two sisters live and move. While their father is alive, he is the male figure of authority and charisma in the community, just as Morten Borgen in *The Word* is the unquestioned head of his family. However, the pastor, in confining his two daughters to spinsterhood, in effect casts a shadow over the rest of their lives. After his death his influence lingers on, crumbling at the edges as the small congregation begins to break up in quarrels. The counterweight to his reformed theology comes from Babette Hersant, eucharistically-minded, an outsider and a woman, who unconsciously sheds a certain ambivalence over this patriarchal ordering. However, since the film ends on a triumphant uniting of traditions and of community, the issue of the merits or otherwise of the dominant father figure is subsumed into the whole.

With *Breaking the Waves*, the third Dane in this chapter, director Lars von Trier, goes for the jugular in order to denounce the
oppression that patriarchal rule engenders. We have moved on
from the temporal distance suggested by the two other films into
the 1970s. This time the location is not Denmark but the equally
remote one of Scotland (the film was partially shot on Skye). The
community is portrayed as introverted, ruled strictly by a patriarchal church. There is a minister supported by the male elders
of the community. Only men may speak during a service and the
church has no bells. Its distinct joylessness is matched by a cruel
theology that in the judgement of the elders, sinners are headed
for damnation. Thus at funerals the minister is prepared to say
of the deceased, 'You are a sinner and therefore consigned to
hell.' There is no fleshing out in the film of a Calvinist doctrine
of the elect (as in the exposition of TULIP in *Hardcore* – see
chapter 6), in which individuals are predestined for heaven and
hell. The focus is only on sin, as judged by the elders, being the
cause of damnation. However von Trier does bring out a major
theme, which is inherent in Calvinism, about the potential
conflict between insiders (locally born) and outsiders (new-
comers) who break the community's rules. His heroine is an
insider who becomes an outsider.

The narrative concerns the salvific power of love which Bess
McNeil, a local girl, exercises over her husband, Jan, an oil worker from the outside. The film opens with their marriage, Bess
losing her virginity to Jan, and then discovering the pleasures of
sexual intercourse before her husband has to go back to his oil-
rig. During this separation, there is an accident at the rig in
which Jan is seriously injured and his life only saved in the operating theatre. However he is completely paralysed. Despite being
warned of the hopelessness of his condition, Bess devotes herself
to him. Because they cannot make love physically, Jan tells Bess
to have sex with others and then tell him about it. This request
leads to, in ascending order of pain: Bess's unsuccessful attempt
to get the doctor in charge of Jan's case to have intercourse with
her; the masturbation of a man on a bus; Bess's metamorphosis

into a prostitute and having sex with the rootless denizens of a gloomy Scottish pub; finally she falls into the hands of a sadistic sailor who takes a voyeuristic pleasure in watching her having sex with another and then disfiguring her with a knife. This journey of degradation is balanced by Bess's unwavering belief that she can keep Jan alive, make him better even, by the power of obedient love. Violated by the sailor, humiliated by the community, and cast out by the church, she resolves to make the final sacrifice: when she makes a second visit to the sailor and dies of her wounds, Jan heals miraculously to resume his life. Before she is buried, he and his mates manage to switch Bess's dead body in the coffin with sacks of sand. Following the interment by the church, during which the minister pronounces her consignment to hell, Jan, back on the oil-rig with the body itself, consigns it to the sea. The next day the oil workers wake to hear the sound of bells in the sky. With Jan in the middle of them, they gaze upwards as if Bess was resurrected in their sound, in defiance of the community's church without bells and in fulfilment of the wish Bess expresses to Jan: 'I like church bells. Let's put them back again.'

In *Breaking the Waves*, the communities of *The Word* and *Babette's Feast* are brought face to face with the modern world. It is not a case of their being softened by the sacramental grace of Babette's feast, but of their values being discredited by the arrival of global economic society in the form of the oil industry. The intrusion of a different world is signalled at the ceilidh after the wedding, when Bob Dylan's 'Blowin' in the Wind' is played on the bagpipes. The stark opposition between old and new is marked as well by the drinking match between Jan's mate, Terry, and one of the patriarchs. Terry downs a can of McEwan's in one go; the teetotal elder downs a glass of lemonade (certainly not champagne) in one; Terry crushes the can with his hand, then the elder crushes the glass. Throughout this ritual they stare at each other.

The principal opposition is between the single young female and the group of male elders. Because it is about miracles, von

Trier's film recalls *The Word*, but he is thinking of Dreyer's *The Passion of Joan of Arc*. Bess is a martyr to elderly intransigence and incomprehension, and at odds with her desiccated mother. Like Joan, Bess is seen much of the time in close-up, and Emily Watson, who plays Bess, has the same wide eyes as Marie Falconetti who played Joan. Like Joan too, she has a pure faith and simplicity that bewilders all around her. In this von Trier also draws on the character of Johannes in *The Word*, believing in the fact of resurrection 'beyond custom and experience' (in the words of David Hume, the sceptical philosopher), that is to say, believing in the existence of miracles. One of the tragedies of Bess's death is that she has embodied the force of life amidst the hardships and damnation-centred culture of the community. She gives life to Jan but only at the expense of her own death. In the end, she is closer to Joan than Johannes.

There is a general opposition between the younger and older generations. When at the beginning of the film an elder asks, 'What good have outsiders brought to the community?' Bess replies, 'Music.' To underline this von Trier starts each of the eight sections of the film with a chapter heading consisting of a landscape shot, enhanced digitally, and on the soundtrack a rock anthem from the late 60s/early 70s, from such luminaries as Mott the Hoople, Rod Stewart, T-Rex, Jethro Tull and others. It is the easy availability of this transatlantic music on radio and gramophone that has been influential in breaking down the walls of the closed community.

The relationship that is a key to understanding Bess is that with her sister-in-law Dorothy, by nickname Dodo. Dodo's husband Sam, Bess's brother, has died young and Bess is the reason that she has stayed 'in this cold place' (not just physically), out of sisterly love and, because she is a nurse by profession, out of a wish to care for Bess who she believes to be 'not right in the head'. Dodo is an outsider from the south of England and brings an English matter-of-factness, an unimaginative rationality to the place. She does attend church but purely because it is the social thing to do and because Bess goes. Yet through the course of the film she gets a glimmer of how Bess's generosity of spirit is salvific (as Babette's had been) and von Trier makes a connection between Bess's words to Dodo, 'Go to Jan to pray for him to be cured and rise from his bed and walk' and Jan's cure. When Dr Richardson finds Dodo on her knees by Jan's bedside, he remarks cynically that his healing would be a 'miracle'; medical science has had to give up. At the inquest into Bess's death, Dodo is present with Jan, now moving about on his own two feet, and Dr Richardson is manoeuvred by the coroner into concluding that in his medical opinion 'the deceased was suffering from being good'. His traditional understanding of medicine has been swept away.

The idea of the good individual being the touchstone by which others around them are judged was given forceful expression in the portrayal of Prince Myshkin in Dostoevsky's *The Idiot*. Bess has the same effect as Myshkin whose attractiveness to women in the novel is reversed in the film by Bess's attractiveness to men. This brings us to the most problematic part of the whole work. What is the relationship between Bess and Jan? Is it a *grand amour* which transcends the lives and communities they live among? Or is Jan manipulating Bess to engage in something very nasty and is Bess too much of an idiot to detach herself from it? Dodo the nurse brings the question up, warning Jan of Bess's susceptibility. When Bess argues that love can save Jan, Dodo tells her, 'sickness is a mighty power' unconsciously echoing and contradicting Jan's counter-assertion that love is a 'mighty power'. For it is how we understand the portrayal of physical love that determines how we judge the film. Cinema is capable of delicacy of touch but throughout much of its brief history film-makers have been drawn to its capacity for grossness, for breaking visual taboos. If *Breaking the Waves* had been a novel, a quite different version of how Bess's surrogate sex affects and sustains Jan could be conveyed: the narrative could be confined to the heads of the two main protagonists. The film on the other hand, especially one constructed to give it a sense of real life taking place before us, is tempted to show the detail of

Bess's experiments. In fact, either von Trier or the censors have exercised sufficient restraint that we are shocked just enough to let our imaginations rip. The film is full of blood: bloodstains when Bess loses her virginity; spurting blood in the operating theatre; Bess laced with blood after her final sexual encounter. This, combined with the knowledge of what Bess is travelling towards when she goes out to the ship a second time, is enough for us to recreate the scene in our mind, without von Trier needing to show it – which he refrains from doing. We are compelled to imagine Bess's degradation, even as we flinch from it.

Paul Schrader's *Hardcore* based its impact on a violent culture clash between the upright religion of Mid-West America and the pornographic hedonism of Los Angeles. *Breaking the Waves* slams together modern and pre-modern culture in the same way. But in *Hardcore* Jake Van Dorn fights and breaks his opponent. Bess does not fight at all, since her only weapon is her own generosity. Her martyrdom is concocted of masochism, an idea that discomforts audiences as much as miracles. Towards the end of the film, Bess is pedalling her moped uphill (the motor has conked out), the local youths are taunting her with, 'You're a tart!', and out of shame her mother will not open the door of her home to her, so Bess struggles towards the church, collapsing before its door. This is her graphic journey to Calvary. From it she sets in motion the path to resurrection. The minister arrives and chases the boys away, but seeing Bess unconscious on the ground in her prostitute's outfit, he turns away in distaste, like the Levite in the parable of the Good Samaritan. Dodo comes on the scene, Bess wakes, and in a moment of tenderness between the two sisters-in-law, she asks Dodo to pray for Jan to be cured. Bess has suddenly become Christ, stepping out to her crucifixion in clear faith as to what her sacrifice can achieve.

The film makes two demands, firstly in its length, which is two and a half hours, and secondly in the way it is shot. In *Joan of Arc*, Dreyer made an extraordinarily fluid film, both with his gliding camera and his rapid cutting. Von Trier takes this fluidity to a new level by using a hand-held camera, which weaves among the characters and is almost a character in itself. As in *Joan of Arc* there are many more close-ups than is usual. While Dreyer's film-making style requires the actors to be movement-perfect, von Trier's hand-held method gives them scope to improvise their movements, their gestures and their facial expressions. This releases Emily Watson, in the part of Bess, to give an extraordinarily emotional performance. Just as Falconetti allows the whole gamut of emotions to cross her face, Watson's expressions and in particular her voice reveal feelings of joy, hysteria, torment and serenity to the limit. Her favoured refuge is the floor of the church, leaning against a pew and having a conversation with God, doing both voices: her own musical voice and with her eyes shut, God's stern patriarchal version. A measure of the relish and conviction that Watson brings to the role is that she persuades us that these conversations are real. Almost as remarkable is Katrin Cartlidge's Dodo, English foil to Scottish imagination, with the film allowing us to penetrate into the intimate relationship the two women have built. At the end when the church elders bury the coffin, which they believe to contain Bess's body, Dodo breaks the rules. For she goes to the graveside, from which females are banned, and denounces the elders: 'You have no right to consign Bess to hell.' From the soundness of this assertion the resurrection of Bess begins as Dodo spots the coffin is leaking sand.

Finally, and most intriguingly, von Trier breaks a rule of film-making, which has almost the status of a taboo: the actor must never look at the camera. Right at the beginning of the film, after Bess has been interviewed by the elders in advance of her marriage and she has affirmed the value of the music which outsiders have brought in, she goes outside. As we watch her in profile, she gives a sly sidelong look at the camera as if inviting the audience to be complicit in her story, in what she plans to do. A little further on, after she has learnt that Jan will be completely paralysed, she sits tearfully by herself in a café and talks to God. In his mouth she puts the words: 'I detest you. Your love for Jan has been put to the test.' At the end, the shot does not end with her looking down, but von Trier holds it as she lifts her tearful face and looks at us. This brief look does more than the earlier shot inviting us to be part of the story; rather it is accusatory, as if we were passing judgement on her. But it is also a revelation of her vulnerability, a weakness which she overcomes by a strength of inner belief in her power to raise Jan from his bed.

11

Heaven

Bring my soul out of prison, that I may give thanks unto thy name: the righteous shall compass me about.

Psalm 142

If we seek heaven on earth, we are not going to find it readily in the films I have discussed in this book, certainly not in the daily life of remote Danish or Scottish communities, not among Bresson's heroes and heroines struggling against earthly discomfort, not in Tarkovsky's epic dissection of the sufferings of the Russian people in *Andrei Rublev*, not in the hardships of life in the American South, not in the imploding Mafia family in *The Funeral*, not in the Los Angeles of Schrader's *American Gigolo*, not in wartime, not at the bedside of a dying person, not on the road to martyrdom. These universes are laden with a sense of sin and earthly pain, more a reflection of what hell might be like than heaven.

Historically, it is out of a wish to use the message of the gospels to recreate in this world the heavenly kingdom outlined there that the monastic movement was born, aspiring to the values of community, mutual love and the worship of God not self. The founders of the monastic orders – such people as Benedict, Anselm, Bernard and Francis – sought a way whereby human beings could live the Christian life at its purest.

In turning away from the anguished world of the films examined in this book, two films about monks celebrate the joy of living on earth reconciled to God in heaven. Both are based on the lives of real people. Both are composed with enormous care, as if the two directors were making a particular personal investment in the films. Both are in episodic form, yet intriguingly their styles are poles apart. In France, when the cinema was invented, the Lumière Brothers and Georges Méliès, whether by accident or in fulfilment of some grand historical purpose one can only speculate, showed how film need not adopt a single mode of representing the world but could be widely divergent. Famously, Auguste and Louis Lumière set up their camera and ran the film uninterrupted for the length of a single roll of film: it might be workers leaving their factory, or a train coming into a station, or the demolition of a wall. While they might have pondered carefully what scene to film and when, the finished result involved a minimum of manipulation. The camera is an instrument to record the everyday life of the world. By contrast Georges Méliès, a magician and illusionist by profession, on seeing a Lumière film and studying the camera as a mechanical device, saw how it could be used to manipulate photographed reality in order to expand his repertoire of illusionist tricks. Thus in the many films he made in the first decade of the cinema he liked to show ghosts, figures appearing and disappearing, disembodied heads and limbs, even a *Christ Walking on Water*. The theatricality of the cinema was emphasised in his sets and costumes and in the extravagant gestures of his actors.

Moving forward 70 years, when Sergei Paradzhanov made *The Colour of Pomegranates*, he not only brought to full flower his belief in the value of art and how the world is enriched by the sacred so that its abundance is inconceivable without it, but he also made one of the finest examples of Méliès-style cinema. Born in Soviet Georgia in 1924, Paradzhanov started his film career with films made in the Ukrainian language. His first notable work was *Shadows of Our Forgotten Ancestors* set in a Carpathian village in the southern Ukraine. His next film, *The*

Colour of Pomegranates, is about the Armenian minstrel Sayat
Nova who became a court minstrel in Georgia. *The Legend of the
Suram Fortress* is a version of a Georgian myth and his last film,
Ashik Kerib is full of references to Muslim Azerbaijan. He thus
can be seen to have worked right at the edges of Soviet film-
making, promoting regional nationalism and asserting cultural
and religious identity.

His choosing to film the life of Sayat Nova in *The Colour of
Pomegranates* can be seen now as a means of mirroring his own
art and the tribulations of making it. Like Paradzhanov,
Haruthiun, who adopted the pseudonym Sayat Nova (King of
Song), was born in Tbilisi in Georgia. After starting life as a
weaver, he composed songs in Armenian, Azeri Turkish and
Georgian, reflecting the ethnic diversity of a region made up of
petty princedoms and dominated by Turkish and Persian over-
lords. He became minstrel to King Irakli II of Kakhetia but after
his wife's death retired to a monastery in 1770. He was killed in
1795 by Shah Agha Muhammad's troops during the suppression
of a Georgian rebellion, having refused to renounce his faith
reputedly with the verse, 'I shall not leave the Church, I shall
not turn from Jesus.' While reflecting the pains and difficulties
of the human condition, his poems delight in love and his
imagery revels in jewels, precious metals, silks and brocades. In
tune with Paradzhanov's homage to Méliès (whether conscious
or unconscious), Sayat Nova is a lover of artifice, both in the
world around him and in the language with which he expresses
it. Since mystery surrounds his departure from the court of King
Irakli, dissidence may have been part of his life as well as
Paradzhanov's, as we shall see.

While initially puzzling, the film comes into focus on repeated
viewings. The film does have a biographical straightforwardness:
it starts with Sayat Nova's childhood and youth, and evokes the
life of the court. The second half of the film concerns his life in
the monastery and ends with him leaving it, meeting the Angel
of Death, and then dying in the monastery itself. Yet the true
flavour of the film, and of the way Paradzhanov has used the

poetry as a springboard to depict the life, may be gathered from the visual opulence of the way certain episodes are narrated.

Throughout the film various texts from Sayat Nova's poetry are quoted. The first of these is: 'Three sacred goals exist: to cherish the pen, the written word and the book.' A tableau is then presented of five monks stacking books that have been waterlogged in a rainstorm, the presence of water being reinforced by the sound of it running. In the child's presence, a monk places a large stone on a pile of books, which squeezes the water from them. The boy then climbs a ladder with a large volume and we see him on the roof making his way among dozens of volumes opened and neatly laid out on the roof of the monastery. We see close-ups of some of the pages illustrated with various gospel scenes including the baptism of Christ, Jesus with his disciples, the Last Supper. Then in an astonishing image, the camera perched high up gives a bird's-eye view of the boy lying flat on his back with the opened books all round him on walls and roofs, their bleached pages turning in the breeze.

Secondly, 'Prayers before the Hunt' shows us a tableau of monks, soldiers and dancing women before a monastery, then a second tableau of men with a lion cub, two peacocks and an antlered deer. Next come prancing horsemen, three women gorgeously dressed, a man with a peacock in his arms holding its beak in his mouth, and the poet with his musical instrument, all to the sounds of chanting and of horns.

Thirdly, when he enters the monastery, Paradzhanov shows a comic scene of 14 monks eating pomegranates (to prominent sounds of fruit being crunched) while Sayat Nova stands disdainfully at the margins. The daily life of the monastery is then explored, both liturgical (the monks' feet being washed in church, the Catholicos, who is the Patriarch of Armenia, swinging a censer) and manual (the treading of grapes, a donkey making the grindstone revolve).

When it comes to Sayat Nova's violent death, Paradzhanov only hints at it, while elaborating the fact of it with dreams and

angels. We are shown a text: 'Tears dimmed my eyes, I was deliri-
ous. May my enemies know such woe.' He crosses himself and
then shows us a golden bowl empty because there is no water in
the stone stoup. We see a fresco of the Madonna and Child, then
a repeat of Sayat Nova gesturing with his empty bowl, followed
by another fresco of rows of naked men. We confront in close-
up a Muslim warrior with a fur hat, then cut to him on a horse
from which he shoots an arrow. The Madonna fresco appears
again but this time, as if hit by the arrow, the image of her face
falls to the ground. Sayat Nova is shown a third time with his
empty bowl, we see the church interior, and then in a final close-
up Sayat Nova leaning back. This ends the episode 'The Poet's
Old Age', and there follow the seventh and eighth, 'Meeting the
Angel of Death; the poet buries his love' and 'The poet's death'.
In this last section there occurs the most striking of
Paradzhanov's lustrous images paraded through this film. In
long shot, against a monastery gable, seven of the monks take
off their black cassocks revealing a white garment underneath.
In the next shot, transported to the roof, Sayat Nova, naked to
the waist, poses atop a gable near the front, while nine monks
stand in an orderly array on the aisle roof behind him, as if they
had all just flown there. When Sayat Nova dies, he lies on the
floor surrounded by candles, with the camera in the roof looking
down on him. White bundles are then dropped onto the floor,
which turn out to be headless white cockerels still flapping their
wings, knocking over the candles and causing feathers to float
upwards. The final text from his poetry reads: 'Whether I live or
die, the crowd will be aroused by my song. I may pass on, yet
from that day a part of me will remain in the world.'

The film takes the details of the poet's life, of the court and of
the monastery and shows them as blessed with abundance. Even
the Muslim warrior shooting at the Madonna is part of a unity
of creation, as though subsumed in its heavenly richness and
strangeness. It is also true that Paradzhanov is a romantic: more
important than anything else is the survival of Sayat Nova's
poetry, and hence by extension Paradzhanov's film, as if to argue

that it is people like them that enrich the earth (as Andrei Tarkovsky thought); the poet/film-maker encroaches on the role of God. The immortality of the soul is equated with the immortality of art. In canonising the poet, the film-maker seems to be doing the same to himself. Despite this solipsism, the film is less a celebration of a single individual than a hymn to a culture and religion, saturated with a sense of the sacred and the beautiful.

With its roots in nineteenth-century romanticism, dissidence has been a twentieth-century condition of which Paradzhanov's life is as good an example as any, for not only did he decline to be part of the central institutions of Soviet film-making, instead creating his films at the margins, not only is his style in opposition to the mainstream mode of telling stories across the world, but he is a true refusenik: in 1973 he was arrested in Kiev on various charges, which included those of homosexuality and of illegal trafficking in religious icons, and served four years in prison. Once released and back in Georgia he was harassed and blacklisted. In 1982 another attempt was made to bring charges, which ultimately failed. As a result the gap between *The Colour of Pomegranates* and his next film, *The Legend of the Suram Fortress*, was 15 years. His dissidence was therefore sustained by great courage, for although burning to express himself he would not compromise his aestheticism for the sake of authority.

On the other hand dissidence need not be solely political. It can take a religious form, as we shall see in the next chapter in discussing Pier Paolo Pasolini; Roberto Rossellini, seemingly an orthodox Catholic, was equally dissident. Although he spent a whole career of film-making parading the virtues of Christianity, at the end of his life he insisted in interviews that he was an atheist. He seems to have distrusted the practice of faith, especially as organised by religious institutions, but was overwhelmed by the 'immense force' of Christianity on the grounds that it pointed the way to freedom of an absolute kind. Rossellini, swimming in the intellectual seas of Marxism in the Italy of the 1940s, deliberately chooses Christianity as his ideology.

Although many film-makers like Rossellini have long careers, and his stretched for 40 years beginning in the late 1930s and produced 87 hours of film time, few are so hard to summarise. He began by making short nature films before making three war films in the Fascist film industry, all with strong Catholic themes and one (*The Man with the Cross*, 1943) set on the Nazi-Soviet front and featuring an army priest as its hero who dies in the thick of battle seeking to bring salvation to children and Soviets. After the Liberation he creates a trilogy about the effect of war on ordinary people (*Rome, Open City, Paisà, Germany Year Zero*). Then came his marriage to Ingrid Bergman and another series of films on how Christian values must be a part of the post-war world (*Stromboli, Europa '51, Voyage in Italy*). There follows a period between the mid-1950s and the early 1960s when his career seems to drift, although it does include a film made in India in 1958, an indicator of his enlarging consciousness of the world. In 1964 he moves in a radical direction that preoccupies him to his death in 1977. He decides to make films for television in the belief that he could thrive under the disciplines of filming on the cheap and in the hope that television could be the educational medium that would transform mass audiences throughout the world. For his subject matter he embarked on making no less than a history of Western civilisation, in which Christian values are a key element, not because they set the spiritual above the material, but because they balance the two. The project includes a six-hour version of the Acts of the Apostles and a film about Augustine of Hippo, which is a didactic and engaging study of a founding father of the Christian church, but also histories of mankind (*The Iron Age*, specifically focussing on human use of the metal, and *Man's Struggle for Survival*, respectively four and three-quarter and ten and a half hours long), the philosopher Socrates (for reason, like love, is a civilising force), Blaise Pascal poised between faith and science, Descartes, and Leon Battista Alberti (the principal figure in *The Age of the Medici*). The one film of this era to receive widespread distribution is *La Prise de pouvoir par Louis XIV*, a clinical account of Louis XIV coming to the throne in France and imposing absolute monarchy and indeed an absolute version of civilisation as symbolised by Versailles. His most controversial film was *Anno uno*, a portrait of Italian politics between 1944 and 1954 focussed on the Christian Democrat leader, Alcide de Gaspari, who led the country in the post-war years: it managed to upset all shades of Italian political opinion including the Christian Democrats who had commissioned the film.

Rossellini's last feature film before he died was *The Messiah*, his version of the gospel story, which, because it comes right at the end of his career, appears to occupy a position of crowning not just his historical project of the last fifteen years of his life, but his whole career as well. Yet this is misleading, for it was just after completing the film that he went on record as being an atheist, adding: 'What is important in Jesus' message is his faith in man.' Rossellini's heart is not in piety but in humanism informed by the gospel's message of love as the basis of human community. He strove throughout his life to illustrate the value of communal interdependence (the Italian word is *coralità*) and it is no surprise to learn that at his death, the contradictions of his life which he balanced so remarkably were reflected in his funeral: this was a church affair attended both by Enrico Berlinguer, head of the Communist Party, and Aldo Moro, one of the leaders of the Christian Democrats.

Rossellini's dissidence was evolved as he searched to unify humankind, but its complexity has still to be grasped. His assertion of atheism has to be squared with his vision of heaven embodied in *Francesco, giullare di Dio* made comparatively early in his career in 1950. This is a portrait in ten episodes of St Francis of Assisi, or rather of his community, for Rossellini always liked to see the great figures of history as part of a group of men and women, not as isolated individuals. Released with the English title 'Francis, God's Jester' it could as easily be called 'Francis, God's Buffoon'. This is partly because he draws not just on *The Little Flowers of St Francis* but also *The Life of Brother Ginepro*, who expresses his Franciscan humility in a gratingly simple-minded, even absurd way. Both Francis and Ginepro exemplify the philosophy of 1 Corinthians 1:27, which Rossellini cites at the opening: 'But God hath chosen the foolish things of the world to confound the wise; and God hath chosen the weak things of the world to confound the things which are mighty.' Thus it is not just Francis' simplicity that the film seeks to extol, but the very irrationality, even absurdity to which Christian love can lead – the brothers in the rain shouting for joy, Francis embracing the leper for sheer love, Brother Ginepro's fearlessness in the face of the brute Nicolaio. In the ninth episode Francis expounds to Brother Leone on what consists 'perfect joy': it is not in making the blind see, not in raising the dead, not in knowing the language of the angels, not in knowing the secrets of nature, not in converting all people to Christianity. It is only after they have been forcibly ejected from the house at which they have sought alms that Francis, sitting in the mud, concludes that perfect joy consists in following Jesus' gift of self-conquest and suffering in his name: 'Only in this is perfect joy.' Rossellini wishes to suggest this idea is not just comic but cosmic as well. Because he films the episodes in the open air of the Italian countryside, because he uses Franciscan novices to play the brothers, because he shows Francis talking to the birds, he makes Francis' world actual. He uses film to embody the imagination that the reader brings to *The Little Flowers* but also uses it to connect the realities of Francis' daily life with Franciscan values speaking down the centuries. To Protestants (never mind atheists), the piety of 'the marvellous encounter between St Clare and St Francis in Santa Maria degli Angeli' is cloying, but when Francis seeks out and embraces the beggar disfigured by leprosy, his compassion is more than reverential but rather a challenge to all individuals of any persuasion.

Perfect joy does not include miracles such as making the blind see or raising the dead. What attracts Rossellini to Francis is the way he conquers suffering and his embracing of poverty (Francis and Poverty were 'lovers', according to Dante in *Paradiso* XI.74). When Brother Masseo asks Francis why the whole world wants to

follow him, Francis replies that God 'could not find among sinners anyone more vile, useless, and sinful than me . . . to employ
for the marvellous work that he intends to accomplish'. In *The
Little Flowers* this episode is set simply as Francis was 'returning
from prayer in the wood' and is a dialogue between the two
monks. Rossellini puts it at the beginning of the film, Masseo asking the question in front of the assembled band of 12
Franciscans, and in a brilliant *coup de cinéma*, it is raining hard,
making the paradox of St Francis' words visible in the incongruity
of expressing the secret of spiritual power on a sodden road.

The early Franciscan literature that survives is largely a parade
of miracles. Rossellini ignores them all. For example, when in
The Little Flowers Francis and Clare meet, 'the folk of Assisi,
Bettona and the surrounding countryside saw Santa Maria degli
Angeli, the whole friary and the wood around it ablaze with
light, as though a great fire were consuming the church'.
Whereas Paradzhanov would have ensured we witnessed this act
of spontaneous combustion, Rossellini films it naturalistically:
the episode concludes with a long shot of monks and nuns sitting in a frozen group. While a voiceover tells us that the people
of Assisi saw the church ablaze, visually it does so only in the
imagination, turning the words into metaphor.

His version of *The Messiah* similarly eschews miracles (even
Jesus' resurrection is a rarefied affair), for he finds the sacred not
in the supernatural but in the everyday. If anything the miracle
is in the way the great people of history lived and worked among
ordinary people. His *Francis* follows a line of thought expressed
most daringly in *The Miracle*, made two years earlier (and
especially consonant with Pier Paolo Pasolini's belief, which will
be explored in the next chapter, in the capacity of pre-industrial
peoples for the sacred). This is a 43-minute film made from an
idea by Federico Fellini, who collaborated with Rossellini on a
number of his scripts at that time including *Francis*, and released
as a segment of *Ways of Love*. A peasant woman, Nanni, is in the
fields when, seeing a man walk past her, she tells herself that it
is St Joseph. She stops him and as they rest, she asks him 'to take

her to paradise'. A voice-over refers to the revelation in the gospel by the angel to Joseph: 'Joseph, son of David, be not afraid to take Mary, for that which is born was conceived.' Waking later, she finds Joseph gone and returns to the village. Nanni is almost without possessions and spends her time hovering around the church. To the villagers she is a madwoman and when she is discovered to be pregnant, she is humiliated by them and made to walk a *via dolorosa* out of the village. Fleeing it she makes her way into the hills and struggles towards a hilltop church, following the path of a goat. The main door is locked, but finding a back entrance and going in, she gives birth to her child. At the end, saying 'my child, my creature, my blood, all mine' she feeds the child at her breast. The creative tension in the film is between the simple facts of the story (a woman gets pregnant through a passer-by, is mocked by the village, and gives birth secretly) and its gospel quality: Nanni's conception is of an immaculate kind, she is shut out by society and church, the birth is a version of the Nativity.

Rossellini is intrigued by the conjunction of poverty and sacredness. Unusually for someone so concerned in his other films to express communal interdependence, he isolates Nanni from her social surroundings in a violent way, and hints at the failure of the Church as an institution to give her shelter: it can only be by the back door. For Rossellini's religious atheism reveals a complex mix of ingrained Catholicism and intellectual rebelliousness. In his way he is the paradigm of a Christianity that urges society to strip away the institutions of the Church and rediscover the essence of Jesus' message.

To sum up, the serenity of heaven is achieved by attaining a new vision of the world. Plato recounts a story in *The Republic* of prisoners being led from the cave where they have spent their lives into the sunlight so that they see the world face to face instead of as shadows on the wall. The same set of data can be interpreted differently. In *Francis, God's Jester*, even in *The Miracle*, there is a peace to be attained in following the spirit of the gospel.

12

The Image of Christ

Christ plays in ten thousand places, lovely in limbs, lovely in eyes not his
    G. M. Hopkins, Sonnet ('As kingfishers catch fire . . .')

A number of the films discussed in this book draw on ideas that occur in the gospel narratives. While those ideas are not unique to the gospels since parallels can be found in the literature of Greece and Rome, as well as in the Old Testament, they are presented there in a vivid, almost supercharged way. Jesus' life still remains a source of inspiration for modern narrative and, as we have seen, for the cinema: crucifixion in *Rome, Open City*, resurrection in *The Word*, salvation in *Pickpocket* and *O Brother, Where Art Thou?*, martyrdom in *The Passion of Joan of Arc*, humility in *Francis, God's Jester*, the imitation of Christ in *Diary of a Country Priest*. The makers of these films draw on the universality of the gospels, unafraid to locate their stories in the modern world. We come now to consider how the cinema has treated the gospel story itself.

To start, take the specific event of the Sermon on the Mount, Jesus' speech recorded in Matthew's and Luke's gospels, beginning 'Blessed are the poor . . .' The words are the important part, not how it was done, nor what it looked like. Yet to show these things visually is to add a new dimension to the way they should be interpreted. The two evangelists specifically mention that Jesus addresses the speech to his disciples (which does not have to mean the narrow group of twelve, but a small number is implied) and Matthew says that he went to the hills 'on seeing the crowds' as if to escape from them. So, there are some visual clues.

The prevailing tradition for illustrating this scene is the one the Americans adopt, as if Jesus was addressing a great rally of people. *King of Kings* gives large weight to the episode, extending the Beatitudes seamlessly into an exposition by Jesus (just as Matthew does) in order to give it a centrality in the film: it lasts 15 minutes. It starts with many people gathering in the hilly, open country (rather as if they were coming to an open-air rock festival). Jesus is alone under a tree, then rises at Peter's call, and while the music becomes diminuendo, he moves to the top of the slope and lifting his arms wide, calls out 'Blessed are you who are poor . . .' He then moves into the crowd and the scene develops into a question and answer session, with the camera staying close to Jesus as he answers questions from the floor: 'Give us a sign . . . When is the kingdom of God coming? . . . What must I do to inherit eternal life?' and so on up to 'Teach us to pray' which leads into the Our Father. There is a long flowing movement to the whole episode underlined by Miklos Rosza's heavy score.

In *The Greatest Story Ever Told*, Christ's speaking of the Beatitudes takes place in the Glen Canyon National Park in Utah and lasts some 90 seconds. Jesus is at the top of a rocky outcrop, ringed neatly by his disciples in two groups of six, while just below a large audience stands stock still: a revelation of an ordered heaven of believers. The camera rises slowly to reveal a glimpse of the huge landscape beyond but this promising movement is not completed. Instead we cut in closer to the statuesque figure of Jesus and the reverential intonation of the Our Father.

Contrasted to this are two Italian versions. In *The Messiah*, which Rossellini shot in North Africa, only a small number of people gather to listen, and on the low African plain, as if deliberately to play down the elevated and mystical quality that a speech on a mountain implies, Rossellini has Jesus stand on a small rocky outcrop. The camera stays largely in the middle distance, an observer at the back of the small crowd. To be present at one of the most influential speeches in the history of mankind is to discover that it is a low-key, seemingly insignificant affair.

Then compare another version, that of Pier Paolo Pasolini in *The Gospel According to St Matthew*. While the Beatitudes are given as a voice-over on the soundtrack, the 40-second sequence begins with a slow pan right over a stony landscape as Jesus and his disciples, a revolutionary cell as it were, walk through it in long shot, the camera then cuts to them moving up a hillside, and ends with a close-up of Jesus' face, connecting the words we have been hearing with their author. Pasolini, following Matthew, adopts the same tactic of leading from the Beatitudes into a series of Jesus' sayings, but uses short lengths of film concentrating on Jesus in close-up and varying the setting: sometimes in full sun, sometimes in twilight, sometimes blown by the wind and so on. Both Nicholas Ray in *King of Kings* and Pasolini have met the challenge of filming a sermon full on but Pasolini by the density of his images is better able to sustain the visual momentum of this episode.

In considering films of the gospels, we find a new dimension is added to the stories described in this book. Filming Jesus' life has plenty of recognisable narrative elements such as a beginning, a middle and an end, a dramatic climax of trial and condemnation, and then a surprise twist right at the close, the resurrection of Jesus from the dead. It has plenty of visual possibilities too: the folk-story of Jesus' birth, various miracles, including the miracle of the resurrection, stories within the main story like that of the prodigal son, and the gritty realism of arrest, torture and death on a cross.

What is new is the 'sacredness' of the story. While all four directors of the films I have mentioned – Nicholas Ray, George Stevens, Pier Paolo Pasolini and Roberto Rossellini – might have wished to come at it afresh, not only have two millennia of Christian art got to be taken into account but millions of people know the story before they have even begun telling it and many will regard any liberty taken in doing so with suspicion verging on outright hostility. At the heart of the problem for the film-maker is that Jesus is both human and divine. How can that be portrayed visually? When Nikos Kazantzakis wrote *The Last Temptation of Christ*, in which Jesus of Nazareth, the carpenter who makes crosses for the Romans, is tempted to lead a life away from the cross with Mary Magdalene, he gave us an interesting novel of ideas. Yet when Martin Scorsese made a film of it in 1988, he brought upon himself the wrath of a section of Christian opinion that regarded the film as blasphemous. Freedom of expression is one of the Western values we cherish but its practice is at its weakest when religious themes are touched on. Film censorship comes in two forms: explicit, as for example in the UK where in the early 1930s depiction on film of the material figure of Christ was forbidden; and implicit, such as the boycott of Scorsese's film encouraged and led by religious leaders.

Painters depicting the key scenes from Jesus' life have had the same challenge and the different streams of faith evolved different styles – compare the majestic serenity of Piero della Francesca's *Nativity*, both rooted in and shaping Italian Catholicism, and *The Adoration of the Shepherds* by Rembrandt, set in an old barn and holding up a mirror to the Protestant masses of northern Europe. At the time of their painting, the two styles reflected their context. Four to five hundred years later, we have the luxury of seeing all the styles side by side and recognising the originality and brilliance of each of them, as if they were parts of a whole.

For the writers of the gospel coming fresh to the story, their focus is on the power of Jesus' teachings, the power of his miracles, the power of his redeeming act, and the power of his divinity. The language for describing these things is often simple and unelaborated. Nor are they distracted by a need to describe what things and people, including Jesus, looked like. Hence the subsequent growth of iconography to fill the gap, the creation of a set of visual rules in how to portray what happened and to direct our response to what happened. In choosing the actor to play Jesus, the film director runs a severe risk if he or she chooses someone with short hair, beardless and of unprepossessing appearance. Of the four Jesuses we have mentioned, three are conventionally handsome (Jeffrey Hunter in *King of Kings*, Enrique Irazoqui in *The Gospel According to St Matthew* and Pier Maria Rossi in *The Messiah*) and Max von Sydow in *The Greatest Story Ever Told*, by his height and the nobility of his features, supersedes beauty with majesty. So, already Jesus is incorporated into the star system, drawn away from our human plane.

But if this happens how is the historical context to be treated? For the two American films, this is barely a relevant question: Jesus is here and now, living in the twentieth century even when dressed in garb which might belong in the first. Pasolini, on the other hand, solves it by making his film in an ancient landscape and by reference to Christian art and music, as if these many layers were the only prisms through which the story can be seen. The three films enter the mythical plane, which the evangelists map out, at the expense of historical veracity. It is Rossellini who in particular seeks to engage with this latter aspect. Interestingly his Jesus is the least 'starry' of the four, and means the film stays more grounded. Secondly, much of it is shot in the middle or long distance. By the end of his career, he developed a style of placing his camera some distance from the action and then using the zoom lens to create visual mobility, zooming and panning towards and away from figures. The camera plays the role of observer and discreet commentator. Thirdly, he is particularly taken with the teachings of the gospel. John the Baptist and Herod have an earnest but civilised dialogue about the opposition between freedom through the exercise of power and freedom through the pursuit of truth (elaborating the relationship between the two sketched in Mark 6:20). The film lasts 145 minutes and the truncated version of Jesus' crucifixion (there is no *via dolorosa*) allows more time for Jesus speaking – to his disciples, to people in the street, and to the priests tailing him. Particularly attractive is the focus on everyday activity. Even during his ministry, Jesus remains a carpenter, fettling ploughs and boats with credible tools and techniques, all the time talking to his disciples. All around him, people are at their daily work, and there is a wonderful counterpoint between Jesus' words, momentous because so influential – we are witnesses to an exposition of ideas and values, Rossellini is saying, that will create a great civilisation – and the ordinariness of daily human business.

Rather depressingly, the furore surrounding Scorsese's *The Last Temptation of Christ* seems to have played a part in making film directors (or the film producers who have to put up the money) wary of tackling the subject. However this caution is nothing new. The advent of the sound film in the late 1920s had introduced new codes of what could be permitted and what not. There was a notable version of the gospel story made in 1927 by Cecil B. DeMille entitled *The King of Kings*, at a time when large-scale epic film-making was in vogue, and prior to that there had been at least 39 earlier versions of the Christ story. But after the advent of the sound film, Hollywood film-makers kept off the subject of the life of Christ for over 30 years, as though it were not suitable for mass audiences in the cinema. It was not until the biblical epic returned to fashion in the 1950s, along with the invention of wide-screen formats, that the taboo was broken and a number of versions followed until *The Last Temptation* appeared. The way had been heralded by two epics, the lives of whose heroes intersected with, and came under the influence of Jesus, namely a Roman centurion in *The Robe* (1953) and a Jewish slave in *Ben-Hur* (1959). Nor is the epic format an accident, since it provides an excellent form for portraying the spiritual journey. It is not just its length, which could certainly be emulated in a novel, but the variety of its scenery, its scope for action and stillness, the way its grandeur can echo the momentousness of what is at stake: nothing less than the purpose of life. *Ben-Hur* uses the Roman Empire as the space in which the spiritual journey can become a heroic one.

Its driving heart is the enmity between two childhood friends: Judah Ben-Hur, the Jew, and the Roman Messala. Judah rejects the argument that Rome is the unconquerable power. There is a hint that he is the leader in waiting, the Messiah whom the Jews expect. But some larger force is at work. Throughout the narrative, the figure of Jesus is like a phantom hand off-screen drawing the events of Judah's life towards the crucifixion on Calvary, the saving moment which heals his mother and sister from leprosy, and heals Judah from his enmity of what Messala stands for: his Jewish family become Christian. This 'presence' works because it is assumed that the audience can make the connection when Jesus is found to be absent from Joseph's workshop, when his hands are shown giving Judah a drink of water on his march into slavery, when Esther talks of the rabbi who preaches forgiveness. Jesus' figure derives divine power from the way his presence is hinted at rather than shown. When towards the end we do see a conventional Sermon on the Mount, Jesus in the far distance standing authoritatively before his audience, our imagination, on which the film has played effectively up to this point, is compromised.

After *Ben-Hur* came a direct assault on the gospel story with *King of Kings* (whose title harks back to DeMille's 1927 film as if to emphasise a continuity despite the 30-year gap). To direct it, the producer Samuel Bronston hired Nicholas Ray, notable up to that point for his ability to probe psychological depths in tough American males, such as Humphrey Bogart in *In a Lonely Place*, Robert Ryan in *On Dangerous Ground*, Robert Mitchum in *The Lusty Men* and James Dean in *Rebel Without a Cause*. Ray and his screenwriter, Philip Yordan, were faced with a problem: how do you give psychological depth to God incarnate, especially when he is to be played by the blue-eyed, all-American Jeffrey Hunter? They solved it by building up the role of Barabbas, committed to violence as a means of overthrowing Roman power, and by counterpointing his message with the pacifist one of Jesus as if they were two halves of the same character. Judas Iscariot then becomes a key link, shuttling between the two camps and trying to resolve in his mind who is to be the true king: Barabbas or Jesus? The result is that Judas retains his human complexity, but plays a comparatively minor role, while neither of the two main protagonists becomes interesting as people.

In fact it is the characters at the edge of the gospel story, like Judas, who can offer a dramatically fruitful way into it. At almost the same time as *King of Kings* was being made, the figure of Barabbas was being given even greater prominence in the filming of the distinguished novel *Barabbas* by the Swedish writer Pär Lagerkvist, published in 1950. Lagerkvist called himself a 'believer without faith – a religious atheist' who shrewdly chose the figure of Barabbas to convey an intriguing form of religious doubt in its most literal form: why should Jesus have died for me, in my place?

The story begins with the release of Barabbas, thief and murderer, in place of Jesus, and with his witnessing of the crucifixion. When he learns of Jesus' resurrection, he goes to find the disciples, Peter among them, to accuse them of stealing the body. Soon after, he is again arrested and sent to serve a sentence of hard labour in a sulphur mine. When the mine caves in, he manages to escape death once again and ends up in a gladiator school. His evasion of death at the hands of a sadistic gladiator leads the Emperor Nero to grant him his freedom, but after his release he is accused of taking part in the burning of Rome, meets Peter again in prison and, finally accepting that Jesus *was* the Son of God, dies on the cross thus exorcising the guilt that had been pursuing him.

While the film is wooden as epic, particularly risible in its depiction of low-life Jerusalem, it has several virtues: it treats the scourging of Jesus in striking fashion, both musically and visually (the scene is based on *Christ after the Flagellation* by Velasquez in the National Gallery in London); the crucifixion was filmed during an actual eclipse of the sun, to brilliant effect, setting in motion a properly biblical theme running through the film of light and dark; there is a thrilling gladiatorial combat between Barabbas and his tormenting opponent who is played to the hilt by Jack Palance, master of the sinister, soundless laugh. Above all, the film is one of ideas: Barabbas is freed from death four times into the presence of brutishness, of suffering and of doubt, in short into an absence of freedom. The film's true end is Barabbas lost in the catacombs of Rome shouting 'Where am I? Show me the way!' The burning of Rome, Peter's homily to Barabbas and then his crucifixion feel like an afterthought.

Barabbas was the brain-child of Dino De Laurentiis, an Italian producer with a taste for epics (witness *Ulysses*, *War and Peace*, *Waterloo*, even *The Bible*), made in Rome with Italian technicians. Almost simultaneously, something else was taking place in Rome on a similar grand scale, the summoning by Pope John XXIII of the Second Vatican Council. In 1958 Pope Pius XII had died and at the age of seventy-seven Angelo Roncalli was elected in his place as John XXIII, apparently as a stopgap. Yet within three months he had summoned an ecumenical council to modernise the church and work for the reunion of Christendom. Although the Council did not open until 1962, it was prepared for by the draft documents produced in Rome of a conservative nature and unofficially by public discussion and theological argument in print. It marked a wish by Catholics to engage with the modern world and how it should be shaped in an era of prosperity and growing technological change. One of the two texts to receive final approval in the second session of 1963 was that on the Instruments of Social Communication, that is the press, radio and TV, but also the cinema. As it happens, this was one of the slightest documents to come from Vatican II but the very recognition of the cinema as a modern means of expression with which the Catholic Church should engage was of some significance.

Whether the calling of the Council, which seems unlikely, or some other impulse persuaded the Italian novelist, poet and film-maker, Pier Paolo Pasolini, to consider filming one of the gospels is not clear. Although preferring John's Gospel, he thought Matthew's would make the better film and had embarked on a treatment during the shooting of *Mamma Roma* in 1962, but immediately after took an apparently contradictory step by filming a satire of 'Hollywood on Tiber' (as the American involvement in Rome's Cinecittà studios was nicknamed, particularly for making films shot in the Ancient World). His 30-minute contribution to a compilation film called *Rogopag* was as follows: in the countryside near Rome, a film director is making a religious epic. During a break in filming the crucifixion, Stracci, the actor playing one of the thieves crucified with Christ, finds a table of food prepared for the cast and crew. Falling on it with the fervour of the hungry, Stracci devours an enormous quantity of ricotta cheese. When filming is resumed, he is lifted up on the cross where, overcome by indigestion, he dies.

The release of the film brought down on Pasolini the wrath of the authorities. A charge was brought against him of vilifying the church and he was given a four-month suspended sentence, only for the penalty to be quashed on appeal. As a Marxist, Pasolini might have been expected to react with some bitterness. Yet he held a deep conviction that modern technocracy was in the process of destroying the human sense of the sacred. In fact he was a 'religious atheist' if ever there was one. With friends on the Catholic left and with 'everything made easier by the advent of John XXIII' he picked up his treatment of Matthew's Gospel and set his mind to showing how a biblical epic really should be created. It was a feature of Vatican II that a tension existed between the official documents produced in Rome and the unofficial Catholic opinions being voiced elsewhere. Similarly, while the maker of 'La Ricotta' tangles dramatically with the official Catholic Church, he not only takes an intense interest in what is being said by Catholics unofficially, but makes his own contribution to the debate, as dramatic as any, by resolving to film Matthew's Gospel. Released at the Venice Film Festival late in 1964, it astounded not only Italian communists that he should have embarked on such a project, but also audiences around the world with the intensity of its conviction. When Pope John called for *aggiornamento* (modernisation) in the Church he might not have envisaged that almost within a year of his death, an Italian Marxist would make a religious masterpiece dedicated to his 'dear, joyful, familiar memory' (the film's final credit is 'alla cara, lieta, familiare memoria di Giovanni XXIII').

What are the qualities of *Il Vangelo secondo Matteo,* in English *The Gospel According to St Matthew* (although Pasolini was strongly irritated by the addition of 'saint')? At first sight it has an astonishing closeness to the text, so that for the Christian believer the sacredness of the book is profoundly respected, but it also is the work of a literary man with a remarkable gift for visual images. In this ability to combine the worlds of words and of pictures Pasolini echoes his Renaissance forerunners such as da Vinci, Michelangelo and Alberti: besides writing novels and poems, he was an intellectual and semiologist, he wrote a book about Italian paintings, he drew (an exhibition of his drawings was held after his death), he had a passion for music. *The Gospel* brings these elements together more than any other of the many creations in the packed 53 years of his life.

In order to visualise the Gospel, he first thought to film it in Palestine but after a visit rejected this as unsuitable, settling instead for the rugged landscapes of Apulia, Calabria, Basilicata and Catania in southern Italy. For Jerusalem he used the old part of Matera near Taranto. This unfamiliar, impoverished Italy is arresting in itself and its buildings made an archaic and intangibly appropriate setting when compared to the papier mâché and plywood buildings of the Hollywood epic. But his creative imagination did not insist on some documentary adherence to the dress of the first century AD (assuming that such dress, whether military, royal or peasant, could be objectively determined). Instead he sought inspiration in painting, especially of the Renaissance: hence the Pharisees' hats and the garb of the Roman soldiers are from the paintings of Piero della Francesca, the pregnant Mary is a Renaissance Madonna and, so Pasolini claimed, 'Giotto and Norman sculpture were in the background.' He even adopts the visual trick of showing people with their bodies foreshortened by the camera (Herod on his deathbed, John in prison) as if the Renaissance fascination with perspective could become the film-maker's as well.

When the film appeared, its music aroused particular admiration, in its variety and its use: the opening of Mozart's 'Dissonance Quartet' for the healing of the leper, breaking into the 'Gloria' from the Congolese *Missa Luba* as the miracle is achieved; the slide guitar of blues-singer Leadbelly whose stretched-out notes exaggerate the shuffling gait of the cripple as he approaches Jesus; for the massacre of the innocents Prokofiev's stabbing music for the film *Alexander Nevsky*; a grave Negro spiritual to solemnise the Nativity. Bach is particularly favoured, including Webern's arrangement for chamber orchestra of the 'Ricercare' from the *Musical Offering*. Pasolini makes explicit use of Bach's *St Matthew Passion*: an orchestral version of the chorus 'Wir setzen uns mit Träner nieder' is used not just at the end as it is in Bach's *Passion*, but at other points as well. The breadth of both the visual and musical references in the film embody Pasolini's intention to tell the story and in doing so, encompass 2000 years of story-telling about the life of Christ.

This mobility of style and of imagination is particularly marked when the film is compared to *The Greatest Story Ever Told*. The release of the latter film in February 1965 was close to the conclusion of Vatican II and appears to reflect the spirit of the Council's aspiration to modernise the church. However, the Vatican imprimatur it aspires to bear, even if it was not officially given, did not prevent it sinking at the box office (having cost $20million to make, it only grossed $8million). Its tone of reverence causes it virtually to freeze, so that its clunking length of 225 minutes derives mainly from the paralysis of actors and of camera before the drama. It has two great virtues. The first is in its use of the desert landscapes of Death Valley and of Utah and Nevada so that at moments when the attention wanders, one can at least gaze in wonder at the scenery. The second is the use of the Swedish actor, Max von Sydow, as Christ. His long bearded face, sleek locks, tall stature and pronounced delivery of the words give Jesus a commanding presence and authority. The whole conception of Jesus is as of someone commanding but distant, in but not of this world.

At the time of *The Greatest Story*, von Sydow was barely known to mass American audiences, so his appearance would have been fresh. Yet even in this respect Pasolini's film produces a remarkable trump card. Looking for an 'intellectual in a world of the poor available for revolution' Pasolini had considered both the Russian poet Yevgeny Yevtushenko and the American Beat writer Jack Kerouac for the role, and then discarded the idea. Indeed he had spent almost a year looking for the right person when a Catalan student, Enrique Irazoqui, coming by chance to see him, found himself cast in the role. 'He seemed to correspond exactly to the picture which I had had in my mind for several months,' said Pasolini afterwards. Under his direction, Irazoqui's contribution is an important part of the film's success. He brings no baggage of previous films to the role (nor indeed of subsequent ones because he never made another film) and fitted perfectly into the long tradition of how Jesus has been portrayed visually, Pasolini being faithful to Christian iconography as well as to the text of the gospel. While von Sydow's face is another static element of a static film, Pasolini manages to vary Irazoqui's face throughout the length of *The Gospel*, by using direct sunlight, through chiaroscuro, through lighting the face at night. Strikingly, in Gethsemane, he uses a special lens to give the face sweating in agony an elongated, El Greco look.

All Pasolini's actors are non-professionals, either faces taken from the street or literary friends. This is quite deliberate. Nowhere was his atheism more religious than when revering the sacred that he professed to find in landscapes, in objects, or in the way in which one person looks at another. He particularly links this idea with the peasantry, which he claimed was the class best placed to serve as the vehicle of revolution. It was in the nature of peasant civilisations, untouched by technological or indeed intellectual civilisation, to take nature and people at their face value, 'not to find nature "natural"'.

Pasolini did not therefore approach the story of Jesus in a neutral manner but as a vehicle for his own ideas. On closer inspection, *The Gospel* is a tendentious version of Matthew, just as Matthew's had been of his original source. While there is fidelity to much of the text, his choice of what not to use is important for an understanding of his approach: some teachings are omitted, such as chapter 19 on marriage; several key parables do not appear, for example the ungrateful servant (18:23–35), the vineyard (20:1–16), the wedding feast (22:1–14); the sending forth of the disciples is glossed over. While some of the healing miracles get in (Pasolini argued for their 'subjective reality'), some do not (the Gadarene swine episode was filmed but rejected as being too horrible). In particular the transfiguration (17:1–8) is jettisoned on the grounds that it showed Jesus' divine transcendence, which was too much for Pasolini's atheism. Curiously, his account of the crucifixion chapter (27) is garbled. The flagellation is omitted; there is no casting of lots for Jesus' garments; no nailing up of 'This is Jesus the King of the Jews'; no mockers; no resurrection of the bodies of the saints which slept (verse 52); no centurion saying, 'Truly this was the Son of God' – all of which offer opportunities to the visual imagination. Instead, Pasolini latches onto verses 55 and 56: 'A number of women were also present, watching from a distance . . . Among them were Mary of Magdala, Mary the mother of James and Joseph, and the mother of the sons of Zebedee' (REB). This becomes an excuse for this group to be witnesses at nearly all stages of Jesus' trial and crucifixion. As he is being stripped prior to nailing to the cross, a woman pushes forward to dab his face – canonical not to the gospel but to the Catholic tradition of the Veronica. Central to the group are two figures from John's Gospel not mentioned in Matthew, that of Jesus' mother Mary, falling again and again in grief in a filmic version of the *mater dolorosa*, and the 'disciple whom Jesus loved'. What is more the old Mary is played by Susanna Pasolini, Pier Paolo's mother, and it may not be fanciful to discern a touch of autobiography in the film: in the uncomprehending but loving sight of his mother, he plays the prophet seeking a kingdom of the sacred and being crucified for it.

Pasolini will remain fascinating to later generations for the extraordinariness of his life and the variety of his achievements. His other films fall into different categories but one unexpected link to *The Gospel* can be made. His first film, *Accattone* (1961, based on his novel *Una Vita Violenta*), is a vivid depiction of low-life Rome.

Accattone (Italian for 'scrounger') is a pimp and petty thief living from day to day on what his prostitute can earn for him and, when he is desperate, from stealing. Remarking that 'he who trusts in providence will never starve', he has a group of friends who are fellow pimps and thieves, all male. He lives among the most marginalised slum-dwellers between city and country, an outcast from his relations. The sight of a funeral procession fascinates him, as though it offered a premonition of his own death. When he is killed in an accident at the end, he lies in the road and says 'Ah, molto bene' ('I'm fine now') as if to say 'It is finished'. There are clear parallels here with Pasolini's version of the gospel story. Jesus lives and works among the very poor, attended by a small group of male disciples. His teaching in Matthew about the family is unequivocal: 'a man will find his enemies under his own roof' (10:36, REB), and it is to a disciple seeking leave to bury his father that Jesus says, 'let the dead bury their dead' (8:21–2). Like Accattone, Jesus and his disciples live from day to day, between city and country. Like Accattone's, Jesus' death is a fulfilment of the life and, just as he was to use Bach's *St Matthew Passion* in *The Gospel*, Pasolini marks Accattone's death with an orchestral version of the chorus that concludes Bach's *Passion*. In particular, he films Accattone as he films Jesus and the disciples in *The Gospel*, full-face, in close-up, seeking to discover the sacredness of appearances.

Yet, being Pasolini, he could not resist making the meaning elusive as well. The denouement of Accattone's arrest and death is filmed with that Italian mixture of realism and operatic force, and to depict the crash, Pasolini does not show us the incident but places it on the soundtrack: a long skidding noise and a scream. Bystanders run, including Accattone's fellow thieves, Balilla and Cartagine. After Accattone's 'molto bene' the camera tracks up to the handcuffed Balilla crossing himself with slow deliberation backwards, 'in utter ambiguity' as Pasolini remarks.

Although *Accattone* was his first film, one of its features is the assurance of its style, even though Pasolini had to learn about the technical aspects of film-making from the beginning. With *The Gospel*, he is still learning, still taking risks and part of the excitement derives from the visual flair to the story, whether in the spare narrative of the nativity or the hand-held, documentary quality of the disturbances Jesus' teaching sparks off in Jerusalem. There is no more dramatic moment in all the gospels than Peter's denial of Jesus at his trial. This incident is a gift to the storyteller: the emphasis switches suddenly from the divine figure to human Peter, frightened, lying through his teeth, and broken by shame. Pasolini, using all his cinematic flair, films the three denials as they come in Matthew in seven spare verses, beginning 'Now . . . But . . . And . . . And . . . And . . .', free of comment, judgement or interpretation. But for the final sentence, 'And he went out, and wept bitterly', Pasolini goes directly for our emotions. In order to create the necessary mood, he shamelessly uses the orchestral introduction to 'Erbarme Dich' from Bach's *St Matthew Passion*, the plangent lament seeking mercy from God that follows the Evangelist's account of Peter's denial. To match this music, the camerawork is virtuosic: it films Peter from the rear, walking quickly away from his tormentors down a narrow street of cobbles, but as he does so the shots lengthen, like a musical rallentando as it were, and when he comes to a halt, the camera rests on his back, the cinematic equivalent of a musical pause. There is a hint of suspense as to what will happen next. When the film cuts to a frontal view of Peter, his face, in close-up now, is crushed in tears. He sinks to his knees and slumps among weeds and stones at the foot of the wall, while the camera pulls back. What is the effect? Is it to convey our revulsion at what has happened, our recoil in horror? The shot is complex enough to include this idea, but its chief effect is to shrink the human Peter so that he seems more abject still. As we reach out to him emotionally, the camera pulls us away. The mind of the film-maker both draws and prevents us, embodying not just our confusion but his own natural humanism as well.

13

Epilogue

Types and shadows have their endings
For the newer rite is here.
Thomas Aquinas translated by J. M. Neale,
Hymn ('Of the glorious body telling . . .')

The central incidents of the gospel story were endlessly reworked
in medieval and Renaissance painting, and a clutch of films from
the twentieth century pick up the challenge of putting this narrative onto film, with images and words experienced in time.
There could have been more. The most notable casualty of the
failure to secure financial backing for his version of the life of
Jesus was Carl Dreyer, who wrote a film script in 1949–50 but
could not find a producer. He felt sufficiently strongly about it to
create a version of the script that was published in 1968, the year
that he died. In fact, Dreyer had already partially tackled the subject in one of his silent films, *Leaves from Satan's Book*, made in
1919–21. The film opens with an injunction from God to Satan
after his fall to 'go out and tempt mankind' (a beginning
reminiscent of the wager between God and Satan in the opening chapters of the Book of Job) and only if he is resisted will he
receive a reduction in his sentence. The film is in four parts, set
in the time of Christ, of the Spanish Inquisition, of the French
Revolution, and in Finland in 1918. In the first three episodes,

Satan's temptations all succeed and only in the last one does he fail when he is resisted by a woman in order to save her husband. The first shows Satan taking the form of a Pharisee in order to tempt Judas to betray Jesus in Gethsemane. Judas is in fact the central figure, so tortured in mind that he comes to temptation almost without knowing why he does so. By contrast Jesus is regal, statuesque in his biblical garments, and his apostles are portrayed as patriarchs rather than as a group of young men. In some ways the depiction harks back to nineteenth-century illustrations of Bible incidents and its hints of Dreyer's gifts as a visual artist, which were to be revealed to the full in *Joan of Arc* less than ten years later, are somewhat tentative, not surprisingly in view of the fact that *Leaves from Satan's Book* was only his second film and the cinema only twenty-three years old. Those hints do include his ability to reduce scenes to their essence, so that the effect is both clear and dignified if (apart from the arresting characterisation of Judas) a bit wooden. Dreyer's desire later in life to make a film of the gospel therefore has the air of his tackling unfinished business.

Reading his script for the projected film gives an unsatisfactory impression of what it might have been like. Dreyer was a master of composition and of camera movement, and thus of ordering the space of his images to intensify the drama he has to unfold. Three features stand out from the script: having included both the resurrection miracles (the raising of Jairus' daughter in Mark and the raising of Lazarus in John), the film ends with Jesus dying on the cross, not with his rising from the dead. Secondly, the interpretation of the story is pro-Semitic. Throughout the film Jewish rituals create the background of Jesus' ministry (something Rossellini makes much of in *The Messiah*) and Caiaphas and Judas are portrayed leniently. The real villains are the Romans, the occupying authority commanded by Pontius Pilate. Dreyer had firmly in mind Cecil von Renthe-Fink, the German minister in Copenhagen from 1940 to 1942, who had initiated the Nazi occupation of Denmark. Thirdly and most strikingly Dreyer's sense of narrative opens the film up by shooting several of the parables as films within the film, such as the good Samaritan, the prodigal son, the ungrateful steward. These sequences allow Dreyer to illustrate the Jewish context of Jesus' life but they are also a naturally cinematic way of illuminating the teaching.

That Dreyer was unable to make this film seems to me to be a signal loss. The cinema has been dominated by the American film industry from the beginning of its history. In 2002 when global box-office revenues came to $18.2billion, films produced or financed in the USA received 83% of those revenues. Yet in a global economy, it is vital that different countries use film to create different identities and the failure to bring Dreyer's version to the screen is a failure of European nerve. Two of Italy's versions of the gospel (*The Gospel According to St Matthew* and *The Messiah*) make a marked counterpoint to those of Hollywood, and there can be no doubt that Dreyer's would have done so as well.

This book has focussed on a number of telling moments from films by a handful of film-makers. There is no more explicit assertion of the non-material than when Inger wakes from the dead in Dreyer's *The Word*. This is a beacon of a spiritual cinema, of showing something larger breaking through the surface of the world: the pool in the Room at the heart of the Zone in *Stalker*, contemplated in silence; the crucifixion in *Barabbas* filmed during an eclipse; in *Mouth Agape* Roger overcome by tears in the presence of his wife's corpse; Francis sitting in the mud pronouncing on perfect joy in *Francis, God's Jester*; in *A Man Escaped*, the prisoners slopping out in prison to the sound of Mozart; and, coming back to Tarkovsky, the swinging of the clapper and as the bell rings out its huge sound at the climax of *Andrei Rublev*, the camera ascending to reveal the crowd of bell-makers and onlookers, some new and perfect creation emerging from the chaos of human existence, the camera both objective observer of this moment of abundance and in its rising, as if on a balloon leaving the earth, passionately caught up in it.

These moments point to stillness outside the stream of life, that there is a dimension in the world outside human narrative. The importance of Bill Viola's videos, like *The Nantes Triptych,* is that the technology allows us to experience time though projected images in a darkened room that is the polar opposite of the frenetic narratives we experience in the commercial cinema. There is a huge area of film-making here yet to be thoroughly explored. In 1970–1 the Canadian Michael Snow made *The Central Region,* in which he mounted a camera in desolate uplands and programmed it by remote control to move at different speeds, in pans, arcs and gyrations round a fixed point. Although difficult to watch because it has no accompanying sound, because it demands three continuous hours of our time, and because its subject is land and sky without human presence, it has an epic quality and creates a visual architecture appropriate to the glory of the creation it seeks to capture. Snow has talked of trying to achieve on film the massiveness of Bach's *Mass in B Minor.*

It is appropriate for a book on religious art, even for a book on cinema, to end with Bach. When he wrote his *St Matthew Passion* in 1727, he was working in a tradition of passion settings that went back several centuries, and flourished particularly in Germany. But his setting is marked by its massiveness and the combining of different ways of presenting the story: the setting of the biblical text is punctuated with arias for solo voices and choral hymns. It is both dramatic and reflective, mixing attachment and detachment. So famous has it become that performance has been lifted away from the church liturgy of Holy Week and often divorced from the religious season for which it was intended. It even features on film soundtracks, Pasolini's *Gospel* and Tarkovsky's *The Sacrifice* being two examples.

We need a reverse movement, a film-maker to film the passion story on an epic scale, but to punctuate its drama with moments of stasis, with commentary, with reflections. The result might be shown in cinemas but even better it might be used liturgically in Holy Week, thus awakening in us a new understanding of this story of stories.

Further Reading and Viewing

The catalyst for this book was firstly the exhibition 'Seeing Salvation' held at London's National Gallery in 2000 and the accompanying catalogue *The Image of Christ* by Gabriele Finaldi and others (London: National Gallery and Yale University Press, 2000), and secondly *Painting the Word: Christian pictures and their meanings* by John Drury (London: National Gallery and Yale University Press, 1999). But the roots for it go much deeper. Since I have been watching films for 40 years, it is difficult to pinpoint when the idea of how the cinema portrayed religious themes began to take hold of me. Seeing Bresson's *Au hasard Balthazar* in a Parisian cinema in 1966 made an enduring impression. I first came across the writings of Amedée Ayfre in his marvellous essay 'The Universe of Robert Bresson' (1964) which was included in *The Films of Robert Bresson* (London: Studio Vista, 1969) and later his *Cinéma et Mystère* (Paris: Les Éditions du Cerf, 1969). He also wrote (but I have not read) *Dieu au Cinéma* which contains a comparison of Bernanos' novel and Bresson's film of *Journal d'un curé de campagne*. Another starting-point was the *Dictionnaire des Cinéastes* and *Dictionnaire des Films* edited by Georges Sadoul (both Paris: Microcosme/Éditions du Seuil, 1965). The entry for *Pickpocket* reads:

> Without a doubt, the film is a paraphrase of *Crime and Punishment*. The director had not thought of Dostoevsky initially, but when he had made the connection, he accentuated the cross-reference. He tells us nothing of the motives that drew his hero towards his 'vocation'. He steals, but without ever making anything of the money or the rifled watches, and he always wears the same shabby clothes. He has no taste for the *acte gratuite* or for living dangerously. He yields to his passion as if to a vice, as if to temptation, as if to sin . . . Would not Bresson also have thought antithetically, of the grace that seizes the sinner 'like a thief'?

I was only twenty when I came across the important interview with Bresson by Godard and Delahaye published by *Cahiers du cinéma* in 1966. Much later came Bresson's *Notes on the Cinematographer* (London: Quartet Books, 1986) and later still the interview filmed in 1965 by Francis Weyergans, 'Bresson ni vu ni connu'.

In writing the book, I have concentrated on the primary materials, the films themselves, and some secondary material, statements by their creators, and hardly at all on the tertiary material, the considerable amount of academic and popular study that has been devoted to the films discussed. Of the secondary material, I single out particularly: *Bergman on Bergman: interviews with Ingmar Bergman* edited by Stig Björkman, Torsten Manns and Jonas Sima (London: Secker and Warburg, 1969), *Pasolini on Pasolini* edited by Oswald Stack (London: Secker and Warburg, 1969) and *Entretiens avec Pier Paolo Pasolini* edited by Jean Duflot (Paris: Editions Pierre Belfond, 1970), *Schrader on Schrader* edited by Kevin Jackson (London: Faber and Faber, 1992), and *Melville on Melville* edited by Rui Nogueira (London: Secker and Warburg, 1971). It is our good fortune that not only have the collected screenplays of Andrei Tarkovsky been published – *Andrei Rublev* translated by Kitty Hunter-Blair (London: Faber and Faber, 1991) and *Collected Screenplays* translated by William Powell and Natasha Synessios (London: Faber and Faber, 1999) – but also the statement of his artistic credo *Sculpting in Time* translated by Kitty Hunter-Blair (Austin: University of Texas Press, 1989) and his vivid diaries *Time Within Time: the Diaries 1970-1986* translated by Kitty Hunter-Blair (London: Faber and Faber, 1991).

It is a scandal that of the 87 hours of film Rossellini made, only some 15 or so are in circulation in Britain. The tertiary literature on Rossellini has therefore been important. Fortunately there are three good surveys of his work: *Roberto Rossellini* by José Luis Guarner (London: Studio Vista, 1970), *Roberto Rossellini* by Peter Brunette (Berkeley: University of California Press, 1987) and *Roberto Rossellini: magician of the real* edited by David Forgacs, Sarah Litton and Geoffrey Nowell-Smith (London: BFI Publishing, 2000). David Forgacs' *Rome, Open City* (London: BFI Publishing, 2000) was also useful. Other studies to be mentioned are *The Films of Carl Theodor Dreyer* by David Bordwell (Berkeley: University of California Press, 1981), which contains a brilliant insight into how Dreyer films the characters in *The Word* ('like billiard balls in slow motion'), *Robert Bresson* by Keith Reader (Manchester: Manchester

University Press, 2000), and *The Night of the Hunter* by Simon Callow (London: BFI Publishing, 2000). *Robert Bresson: a spiritual style in film* by Joseph Cunneen (London: Continuum) appeared in 2003.

For general background, *The Oxford Companion to Christian Thought* (Oxford: OUP, 2000) has been invaluable. Also, the internet site, www.imdb.com, has a wonderful database of cast and crew lists, dates etc. for films from across the world. Through it I came across two essays: one is a survey of films about Joan of Arc, 'Joan of Arc: the cinema's immortal maid' by Tony Pipolo on britannica.com. It contains the vital observation that transfers of *The Passion of Joan of Arc* to video and DVD at 24 frames per second ignores the fact that it was shot at the much slower speed of 16–18 frames per second so that our usual viewing experience is too accelerated. The second is on *Breaking the Waves* by Jonathan Rosenbaum (www.chireader.com), which links von Trier to Dreyer. There is *The Journal of Religion and Film* on the internet, through www.unomaha.edu/~wwwjrf which gives a good indication of the diversity of approaches to the subject. It is edited by William L. Blizek of the Department of Philosophy and Religion at the University of Nebraska at Omaha. I have written in the journal *Theology* about the Kierkegaardian background to *The Word* (January/February 2001) and Pascal's ideas about grace in *A Man Escaped* (April 2002).

For the gospel films, there is a helpful essay 'Jesus Christ Movie Star: the depiction of Jesus in the cinema' by William R. Telford, included in *Explorations in Theology and Film* edited by Clive Marsh and Gaye Ortiz (Oxford: Blackwell Publishers, 1997). Charles Barr put me onto an excellent Ph.D. thesis in the library of the University of East Anglia by Miles Booy 'The Torn Curtain: narrative and authority in the Jesus film' (1997). Dreyer's screenplay for a film of the gospel was published as *Carl Theodor Dreyer's Jesus* (New York: The Dial Press, 1972). I have not been able to get hold of *Letters about the Jesus Film: 16 years of correspondence between Carl Th. Dreyer and Blevins Davis* edited by M. Drouzy and L. N. Jorgensen (Copenhagen: University of Copenhagen Press, 1989).

How easy is it to see the films discussed in this book? Living in London with access to the National Film Theatre is an advantage. For those without it, all the films (except *The Messiah*, *The Miracle* and *The Nantes Triptych*) have appeared on TV at one time or another since the mid-1980s. However, having appeared they have mostly since disappeared. Fortunately the growth of video and DVD sales make it

possible to compensate for this. Virtually all the films can be purchased (e.g. through MovieMail www.moviem.co.uk or Chartbusters
Video www.findthatfilm.co.uk), even Rossellini's *Messiah* which, after 20
years of searching, I tracked down through a link from imdb.com
to the Amazon website. It is a German version without subtitles but it
was an enormous advance to be able to acquire even this.

Filmography

A Man Escaped: Robert Bresson, France, 1956

A Married Woman: Jean-Luc Godard, France, 1964

Accattone: Pier Paolo Pasolini, Italy, 1961

Acts of the Apostles: Roberto Rossellini, Italy, 1969

The Age of the Medici: Roberto Rossellini, Italy, 1973

Al Capone: Richard Wilson, USA, 1959

Alexander Nevsky: Sergei M. Eisenstein and Dmitri Vasilyev, Soviet
  Union, 1938

American Gigolo: Paul Schrader, USA, 1980

Andrei Rublev: Andrei Tarkovsky, Soviet Union, 1969

Angels of the Streets: Robert Bresson, France, 1943

Anno Uno: Roberto Rossellini, Italy, 1974

The Apostle: Robert Duvall, USA, 1997

The Army in the Shadows: Jean-Pierre Melville, France/Italy, 1969

Ashik Kerib: Sergei Paradzhanov and Dodo Abashidze, Soviet Union,
  1988

Au hasard Balthazar: Robert Bresson, France/Sweden, 1966

Augustine of Hippo: Roberto Rossellini, Italy, 1972

Babette's Feast: Gabriel Axel, Denmark, 1987

Baby Face Nelson: Don Siegel, USA, 1957

Bad Lieutenant: Abel Ferrara, USA, 1992

Barabbas: Richard Fleischer, Italy, 1962

Battleship Potemkin: Sergei M. Eisenstein and Grigori Aleksandrov,
  Soviet Union, 1925

Ben-Hur: William Wyler, USA, 1959

The Best Intentions: Bille August, Sweden/Germany/UK/Italy/France/
  Denmark/Finland/Norway/Iceland, 1992

The Bible: John Huston, USA/Italy, 1966

Bicycle Thieves: Vittorio De Sica, Italy, 1948

The Big Heat: Fritz Lang, USA, 1953

Blaise Pascal: Roberto Rossellini, Italy/France, 1971

Bonnie and Clyde: Arthur Penn, USA, 1967

Breaking the Waves: Lars von Trier, Denmark/Sweden/France/Netherlands/ Norway, 1996

Brighton Rock: John Boulting, UK, 1947

Brothers in Law: Roy Boulting, UK, 1957

Carlton-Browne of the F.O.: Roy Boulting, UK, 1959

Cartesius: Roberto Rossellini, Italy, 1974

The Central Region: Michael Snow, Canada, 1970 (installation)

Le Cercle rouge: Jean-Pierre Melville, France/Italy, 1970

Christ Walking on Water: Georges Méliès, France, 1899

The Colour of Pomegranates: Sergei Paradzhanov, Soviet Union, 1968

Day of Wrath: Carl Theodor Dreyer, Denmark, 1943

Le Deuxième souffle: Jean-Pierre Melville, France, 1966

Diary of a Country Priest: Robert Bresson, France, 1951

Le Doulos: Jean-Pierre Melville, France/Italy, 1961

Elmer Gantry: Richard Brooks, USA, 1960

Europa '51: Roberto Rossellini, Italy, 1951

The Exterminating Angel: Luis Buñuel, Mexico, 1962

Fanny and Alexander: Ingmar Bergman, Sweden/France/West Germany, 1982

Francis, God's Jester: Roberto Rossellini, Italy, 1950

The Funeral: Abel Ferrara, USA, 1996

Germany Year Zero: Roberto Rossellini, Italy/Germany/France, 1947

The Godfather: Francis Ford Coppola, USA, 1972

The Godfather: Part II: Francis Ford Coppola, USA, 1974

The Gospel According to St Matthew: Pier Paolo Pasolini, France/Italy, 1964

The Greatest Story Ever Told: George Stevens, USA, 1965

Hardcore: Paul Schrader, USA, 1979

Heavens Above!: John and Roy Boulting, UK, 1963

I Am a Fugitive from a Chain Gang: Mervyn LeRoy, USA, 1932

I'm All Right Jack: John Boulting, UK, 1959

In a Lonely Place: Nicholas Ray, USA, 1950

The Iron Age: Roberto Rossellini, Italy, 1964

Ivan's Childhood: Andrei Tarkovsky, Soviet Union, 1962

The King of Kings: Cecil B. DeMille, USA, 1927

King of Kings: Nicholas Ray, USA, 1961

The Ladies of the Bois du Boulogne: Robert Bresson, France, 1945

The Last Temptation of Christ: Martin Scorsese, USA, 1988

Leaves from Satan's Book: Carl Theodor Dreyer, Denmark, 1921

The Legend of the Suram Fortress: Sergei Paradzhanov and Dodo
  Abashidze, Soviet Union, 1984

Little Caesar: Mervyn LeRoy, USA, 1931

Lucky Jim: John and Roy Boulting, UK, 1957

The Lusty Men: Nicholas Ray, USA, 1952

Mamma Roma: Pier Paolo Pasolini, Italy, 1962

Man's Struggle for Survival: Roberto Rossellini, Italy/France/Romania/Egypt,
  1969

The Man with the Cross: Roberto Rossellini, Italy, 1943

Master of the House: Carl Theodor Dreyer, Denmark, 1925

The Messiah: Roberto Rossellini, Italy/France, 1976

Mirror: Andrei Tarkovsky, Soviet Union, 1975

Money: Robert Bresson, France/Switzerland, 1983

Mother and Son: Aleksandr Sokurov, Germany/Russia, 1997

Mouth Agape: Maurice Pialat, France, 1974

The Nantes Triptych: Bill Viola, USA, 1992 (installation)

The Neon Bible: Terence Davies, UK, 1995

The Night of the Hunter: Charles Laughton, USA, 1955

Nostalgia: Andrei Tarkovsky, Italy/France/Soviet Union, 1983

O Brother, Where Art Thou?: Joel and Ethan Coen, USA, 2000

On Dangerous Ground: Nicholas Ray, USA, 1952

Ossessione: Luchino Visconti, Italy, 1943

Paisà: Roberto Rossellini, Italy, 1946

The Passion of Joan of Arc: Carl Theodor Dreyer, France, 1928

Pickpocket: Robert Bresson, France, 1959

Pierrot le fou: Jean-Luc Godard, France/Italy, 1965

Point Blank: John Boorman, USA, 1967

La Prise de pouvoir par Louis XIV: Roberto Rossellini, France, 1966

Private's Progress: John Boulting, UK, 1956

The Public Enemy: William A. Wellman, USA, 1931

Raising Arizona: Joel and Ethan Coen, USA, 1987

Rebel Without a Cause: Nicholas Ray, USA, 1955

The Robe: Henry Koster, USA, 1953

Rogopag, segment 'La Ricotta': Pier Paolo Pasolini, Italy/France, 1963

Rome, Open City: Roberto Rossellini, Italy, 1945

The Sacrifice: Andrei Tarkovsky, Sweden/UK/France, 1986

Le Samouraï: Jean-Pierre Melville, France/Italy, 1967

Scarface: Howard Hawks, USA, 1932

Shadows of Our Forgotten Ancestors: Sergei Paradzhanov, Soviet Union, 1964

Le Silence de la Mer: Jean-Pierre Melville, France, 1947

Smiles of a Summer Night: Ingmar Bergman, Sweden, 1955

Socrates: Roberto Rossellini, France/Italy/Spain, 1970

Solaris: Andrei Tarkovsky, Soviet Union, 1972

Stalker: Andrei Tarkovsky, West Germany/Soviet Union, 1979

Stromboli: Roberto Rossellini, Italy, 1949

Sullivan's Travels: Preston Sturges, USA, 1941

The Sun Shines Bright: John Ford, USA, 1953

Taxi Driver: Martin Scorsese, USA, 1976

The Trial of Joan of Arc: Robert Bresson, France, 1962

Ulysses: Mario Camerini, Italy/USA, 1955

Under Satan's Sun: Maurice Pialat, France, 1987

Underworld: Josef von Sternberg, USA, 1927

Underworld U.S.A.: Samuel Fuller, USA, 1961

Un flic: Jean-Pierre Melville, France/Italy, 1972

Voyage in Italy: Roberto Rossellini, France/Italy, 1953

War and Peace: King Vidor, Italy/USA, 1956

Waterloo: Sergei Bondarchuk, Italy/Soviet Union, 1970

Ways of Love: Marcello Pagliero and Roberto Rossellini, Italy, 1948

White Heat: Raoul Walsh, USA, 1949

Wild River: Elia Kazan, USA, 1960

Winter Light: Ingmar Bergman, Sweden, 1963

The Word: Carl Theodor Dreyer, Denmark, 1955

Indexes

INDEX OF RELIGIOUS AND PHILOSOPHICAL REFERENCES

INDEX TO ASPECTS OF FILM STYLES